EDWIN P. HOYT served in the U.S. Army Air Corps and in the Office of War Information before he became a war correspondent for United Press International. He also worked for both the *Denver Post* and the American Broadcasting Company in the Far East, Europe, and the Middle East in the years following World War II. Hoyt is the author of many military history books, including *The Men of the Gambier Bay*, *McCampbell's Heroes*, *Bowfin*, *The Sea Wolves*, *The Carrier War*, and *Leyte Gulf*, as well as the War in the Central Pacific series: *Storm Over the Gilberts*, *To the Marianas*, and *Closing the Circle*.

D1003012

RAIDER
16

EDWIN P. HOYT

AVON BOOKS ◆ NEW YORK

All photographs in the insert are courtesy of Ernst Mohr

AVON BOOKS
A division of
The Hearst Corporation
105 Madison Avenue
New York, New York 10016

First Avon Books Printing: August 1988

AVON TRADEMARK REG. U.S. PAT. OFF. AND IN OTHER COUNTRIES, MARCA
REGISTRADA, HECHO EN U.S.A.

Printed in the U.S.A.

K-R 10 9 8 7 6 5 4 3 2 1

To Bernhard Rogge
who accomplished one of the great feats
in the annals of the sea

CONTENTS

CHAPTER ONE

The Problem

Historically speaking, Germany has always been a land power rather than a sea power, although many staunch sailors have been born along the North and Baltic seacoasts, and have braved the seas in all conditions of peace and war. Until the last years of the nineteenth century and the unification of the German states, there was no Germanic navy to speak of, but with Prince Bismarck and Kaiser Wilhelm I came the growth of empire, on land and overseas—and a navy was born.

In the early years that navy was of a very special kind, with its own peculiar operational necessities. The backbone of the German navy in the nineteenth century was the Kreuzergeschwader, the cruiser squadron, whose components might be scattered from the east coast of Africa to the Mariana Islands, showing the Imperial German flag and enforcing the laws of his Imperial Majesty where that flag was flown. Germany embarked late in the nineteenth century on a course of overseas empire that led her to develop far-flung colonies east and west, and the navy was an important instrument of colonial policy.

From the cruiser squadron came the idea of the cruiser operation against enemy shipping, *Kaperkrieg*—what the French did so well under the name of *guerre de course*—and this concept of surface raiders was deeply instilled in the German naval heritage, even before World War I. When that great European struggle began, Germany had developed a High Seas Fleet to counter the British Home Fleet, but except for the indecisive action at Jutland the High Seas Fleet spent the war in maneuvers in home waters and did not go into battle as a unit.

In World War I, the Germans proved the effectiveness of the

1

submarine as a commerce raider, but the submarine was neither first nor alone in that field within the German navy. The first great commerce raider of the war was the light cruiser *Emden*, which sank some 83,000 tons of British and Allied shipping in the first months of the war, also doing away with a Russian cruiser and a French destroyer in the process, before she was trapped at the Cocos or Keeling Islands by the Australian heavy cruiser *Sydney*, battered into submission, and run aground on a rocky islet. *Emden*'s exploits in the Indian Ocean—then regarded as a British lake—brought fame and glory to the whole German navy, and the German nation cheered. Then came, in rapid succession, the exploits of a whole fleet of German commerce raiders, naval vessels, and converted steamers, which preyed on British shipping, particularly in the Atlantic and Pacific Oceans. The *Kreuzerkrieg* or cruiser warfare did more than sink British merchant vessels. The particular type of warfare waged caused the British to tie up scores of naval vessels in search of various German raiders. Vice Admiral Graf Maximilian von Spee, for example, had the British navy on edge for months while he ranged across the Pacific Ocean from the Carolines, bombarded Papeete, knocked out a radio station, destroyed a British squadron at Coronel off the Chilean coast, and then went to his death and the destruction of his own East Asia Cruiser Squadron in the brief, bloody battle of the Falkland Islands.

Another German cruiser, the *Karlsruhe*, operated off the Americas, again causing much trouble to the British defenders, until the German ship blew up unexplainedly one day on the high seas, victim of a mine or her own munitions. And in Africa, the *Königsberg* sortied to the edge of the Indian Ocean, sank a British steamer there, moved to Zanzibar and destroyed a British cruiser, the *Pegasus*, then went into hiding in the Rufiji River delta where she was found and bottled up by the British. But what cost the *Königsberg* was to England! At one time some two dozen vessels were tied up trying to fish *Königsberg* out of that river or sink her, and His Majesty's government expended millions of pounds before *Königsberg* was destroyed.

Aside from the warships and the submarines, whose value as commerce destroyers was quickly proved in the early days of the war, the Germans made use of auxiliary cruisers. At first these were huge passenger liners, fast and strong. *Prinz Eitel Friedrich*, *Kronprinz Wilhelm*, *Kaiser Wilhelm der Grosse* were a few of them. But the Germans quickly learned that the big liners were too distinctive, and they burned too much coal to be effective raiders in oceans that were largely controlled by the enemy—and where Germany did not have a single operating base outside home waters.

By the end of 1915, Germany was no longer using light cruisers in attacks on commerce, for with the exception of those of the main fleet, all the light cruisers were gone. She was not using passenger vessels, for all those had been captured, sunk, or run to harbor at home or in neutral lands. And yet the idea of the surface raider did not die. Out went small, disguised merchant ships with breakaway bulkheads and false funnels and all the devices to fool the enemy, ships that carried 150 mm. guns, torpedo tubes, and mines. Among the most successful of these were *Moewe*, *Wolf*, and *Seeadler*, which among them did away with some 300,000 tons of British shipping. Together, the surface raiders established a proud tradition for the German navy that was unmatched in modern times by any other nation. Germany's naval might was destroyed at war's end by the rebellion within the fleet and by the Treaty of Versailles, but the tradition did not die.

In the years between the wars, Germany's revival of a navy was a slow process. Germany watched, but did not participate, when the big powers met at the Washington Naval Conference in 1922 and agreed to limit the size of individual warships (battleships 40,000 tons complete) and the number of ships of each fleet—in an attempt to stop a naval arms race. From this agreement and the later London agreement of 1930 came some important changes in the building of warships—but again these changes only later affected a Germany that was still barred from arming itself. The Germans watched, waited, and studied.

In particular at this time, the Germans studied the matter of communications, in which rapid strides were being made by the big powers. Germany had suffered sorely from bad communications during World War I. *Emden* was lost because she intercepted fleet messages from the British convoy of which *Sydney* was a part, and assumed from the strength of the messages that *Sydney* was three or four times as far away from Cocos-Keeling as she was in fact on the eve of *Emden*'s invasion of that communications center.

Königsberg's plight was infinitely worsened when the rescue ship *Rubens*, a 6,000-ton freighter, was run to ground and wrecked because the British intercepted communications between *Königsberg* and the supply ship.

The Germans never forgot these lessons, and in the period between the wars when they could not build ships, they could and did perfect their communications system. They could locate ships by their broadcast of radio signals, and could monitor the radio messages. But so could the enemy. The Germans learned to observe radio silence very completely up to the time of contact with the enemy. And higher commanding officers adopted a policy of directing operations from command stations ashore, using blind radio transmissions. The coding machines the Germans developed were so effective that the enemy was unable to decode the messages (as had been the case with *Königsberg*, where her naval code was broken in London after the messages to *Rubens* were intercepted). The Germans also developed means of radio reconnaissance, monitoring radio traffic, decoding messages, and getting bearings on transmitters quickly. By the beginning of World War II the Germans were far ahead of the Allies in radio communications, and this fact had an important bearing on the story of the ship that would be known as *Raider 16*.

Late in the 1920's, when Germany was permitted some warship building, she had turned to the concept of the pocket battleship—once again giving new importance to the commerce raider.

As Germany threw off the shackles of the Versailles Treaty and continued to expand her military might under Adolf Hitler, her admirals advocated the building of a strong navy, but one based on alliance with Britain. Then, in 1938, Hitler informed Admiral Erich Raeder that he considered Britain to be one of his possible enemies. Raeder submitted two alternate plans for the expansion of the German fleet. The first plan called for the building of pocket battleships and submarines, which would be used to destroy commerce. The second plan called for the building of a large German fleet for offensive operations against British naval forces. Hitler accepted the second plan, knowing it would take much longer to develop than the first one, and assured the admirals that he would not need a fleet until 1946. Then, however, almost as quickly as he had made this commitment, the Führer of the German Reich forgot about it. The Z Plan, as it was called, was put into force, but the German navy was not to have time to develop the plan before the fleet was called into action.

CHAPTER TWO

Interlude

In the summer of 1939, a tall, pleasant-faced Fregattenkapitän or commander of the German navy took the sailing ship *Albert Leo Schlageter* on a training cruise to South America. The captain was Bernhard Rogge, a career officer in the German navy, one of that handful who had been left over from World War I.

Rogge had come up through the officers' ranks. A Schleswig-Holstein man, he had been made ensign in the Imperial Navy in 1915, into that old navy whose ways were so hard on the enlisted men, so gentlemanly for the officers. He had lived through the hard times, the uprising, the confusion, the searing years of defeat and degradation. He had served aboard the battle cruiser *Moltke*, and aboard the light cruisers *Stralsund* and *Pillau*. He had learned his profession well, and by 1930, as a lieutenant, he had been given charge of midshipmen training on board the new cruiser *Emden*. There was a voyage one would long remember—a year-long trip to India, Japan, and Africa, where one could forget the miseries of depression-torn Europe and bask on coral sands. He had been executive officer on the *Karlsruhe* in 1935 and 1936 when she went around the world.

Later in the 1930's he had been given command of the training ship *Gorch Fock*. Universal conscription had been reinstated in Germany in 1935 under Hitler, and the building of naval and military machines was beginning again. With so small a navy it was unthinkable that ships of the fleet could be used for training, but the navy had to be reconstituted: hence the sailing ships, grand training vessels in the old tradition where a youngster really learned to find his way about the sea.

5

This was a new navy, this German navy of the 1930's. No
longer were the men subject to the treatment that landowners
showed their peasants in the old days. The officers were middle
class, for the most part, and the concern of the admirals of this
new navy was to teach officers and petty officers the proper
handling of subordinates. Indeed, writing later of this period,
German Vice Admiral Friedrich Ruge noted that "the most
careful attention" was given to this aspect of navy life. Gone
were the days of iron discipline when, for example, during the
battle of the Falklands the first officer of the cruiser *Gneisenau*
shot down a sailor who was absent from his post, having moved
to the scuttlebutt for a drink of water during the long fight. Gone
were the days of chains and harsh punishments. There was
discipline, but discipline based on reason, and opportunity for
promotion and other satisfactions that had been denied the men
of the old German navy, where a petty officer or enlisted man
had no chance of ever achieving officer's rank.

After the *Gorch Fock*, Rogge had been given the *Albert Leo
Schlageter* and enjoyed another of those sunny years in the West
Indian and South American waters. He brought *Albert Leo
Schlageter* and a seasoned group of sailors back to Germany at
the end of June, and was more than a little dismayed to see the
change in atmosphere in the Germany he had left before the
Sudeten crisis. The people in the streets were upset—*"hektisch
und nervös,"* Rogge said—and the tension of war fear was in
the air.

In this month ashore, Bernhard Rogge watched and listened
and said little, for he was a career officer in the German navy,
not a member of the Nazi Party or any of the state subsidiaries
of that party, and professionals kept their opinions on politics to
themselves. He did not dare to believe there would be a war—
so unthinkable was it—but on the other hand . . .

Fregattenkapitän Rogge was scheduled to leave again at the
end of July on a training cruise, this time with an entirely new
crew of petty officer cadets, to journey to Heilegendamm,
Oderbank, and Swinemünde. Before the ship pulled out, he
made a personal journey to the fleet personnel office, to check
on his possible assignment in case of hostilities. There he
discovered that he was scheduled to command an SHK II, a
Schwerer Hilfskreuzer as it was to be called, a larger, faster,
more technically perfect version of the old *Moewe* and *Wolf*

which had terrorized the seas during World War I. The German naval staff had not forgotten the role of the surface raiders dressed as merchantmen. They were picking from strength in their officers' corps to find the men who would take these special ships to sea. It was patently one of the most exciting jobs, offering command, daring, excitement, and above all action against the enemy from the beginning of the war, if it came.

So Fregattenkapitän Rogge came down from headquarters happy in the thought that he *had* a fine assignment on his beloved sailing ship, but that if he were to be parted from her by events, he would have one of the creamiest of the war assignments for men of his rank.

Off they went, sails pulling, yards creaking, and the wind rustling through the rigging of the *Albert Leo Schlageter* in the fine weather of the Baltic of July. But a month after they sailed, the fine communications system of the Admiralty hailed Captain Rogge and his sailing ship, and ordered them to turn about immediately and head for Kiel. The reason: "enemy" submarines had been seen in the Baltic, and it was time to come home.

It was August 25, 1939.

CHAPTER THREE

The Making of a Raider

Fregattenkapitän Rogge and the *Albert Leo Schlageter* did not get back to Kiel before the war broke out. On September 1, Rogge was suddenly informed that as of six o'clock in the morning the German *Wehrmacht* would "return the enemy's fire" and if this was euphemism for Hitler's decision to march into Poland, it meant war nonetheless. Two days later, Germany was also at war with England, and as far as the navy was concerned, the die was cast for a long and intensive struggle.

Among the officers of the regular navy, Fregattenkapitän Rogge was fortunate in knowing his wartime assignment—or that was how it seemed. Indeed, on paper the Seekriegsleitung was totally efficient: Rogge knew enough to call the authorities in Bremen, where his auxiliary cruiser was supposed to be fitting out.

But when Bremen answered, no one there knew anything about a Fregattenkapitän Rogge or an auxiliary cruiser to which he was supposedly posted. (*"Hier ist kein schiff für sie!"* There is no ship for you here!)

And so the tall, beak-nosed Rogge decided to go to Bremen to see for himself, sort out the confusion, and find the Hansa liner *Goldenfels*, a 7,862-ton vessel of 17 knots, which was to be his wartime command.

Very conscious of the injunctions posted everywhere about spies and the dangers of leaking information unguardedly, Commander Rogge took off his uniform and donned civilian clothes to make the trip to Bremen, where he would be scouting around the docks. He found his ship sitting at a civilian pier and made arrangements for her to be moved into the naval dockyard for the process of converting a simple freighter into a ship of war. Then he went to naval headquarters at Bremen to begin the process of assembling officers and a crew.

Secrecy? He discovered that at the personnel office someone had put out a set of identity cards for the new crew of his vessel, each card marked in heavy black letters *Schweren Hilfskreuzer II*, which was as good as announcing that the men were joining a heavy auxiliary cruiser or future raider of the seas!

Quickly Rogge had the men to whom these cards were issued transferred to the privacy of the Petty Officers Training School at Bremerhaven, and instead of the heavy black ink that would tell the world what he was about, he adopted the simple cognomen *Ship 16* for his new command.

For his own part, the tall captain adopted a plain dark suit, a derby hat, and—when the weather grew cold enough for it— a heavy black double-breasted overcoat and white silk scarf. He was dapper, but he looked nothing like an officer in the Reich's navy; he might be a businessman or he might be a merchant captain so far as appearances were concerned. He took up quarters in the Hotel Columbus in Bremen, as any civilian captain might, and began poking around the docks and visiting the naval headquarters to straighten out the problem he considered vital above all: that of picking officers and crew who would be absolutely amenable to his commands and to one another. Fregattenkapitän Rogge, black derby or no, was a professional who knew precisely what he was getting into and what was expected of him. He made it a point to look up officers who had served in World War I on the old raiders, and to discover their problems and their manner of meeting them. He learned that his own procedure was correct: crew was everything on this kind of voyage.

Headquarters had allocated twenty officers to the ship. Rogge's task was to sort them out, and see just what he thought of the personnel officer's selection of men to go out unprotected into deep water, surrounded by enemies, to fight Germany's battle.

There were difficulties. He received a very competent executive officer, Kapitänleutnant zur See Kühn, and a gunnery officer, Oberleutnant Kasch; obviously they knew their business; they ought to, both were from the regular navy. So were several of the junior officers, Lieutenants Strecker, Wenzel, Fehler, and Flying Officer Bulla, for example. The navigation officer, Captain Kamenz, was a merchant captain in his own right, and the ship was assigned a handful of merchant officers, each bearing a master's or a mate's certificate, who held the rank of Leutnant zur See in the regular navy and were classified as Sonderführer. They would be the prizemasters, the men who would steam home with enemy ships bearing precious cargo to feed the German war machine.

Not all the officers were right for the ship, however, as Rogge learned when he was given as adjutant a reserve officer whose main claim to naval fame was hard to determine: in private life he was an art historian.

Rogge went to Fregattenkapitän Winter, chief of officer appointment at Wilhelmshaven headquarters, and persuaded Winter to take back his art historian, plus two reserve officer cadets, in exchange for an officer who might handle the delicate task of running the personnel section of his ship and doing all those other odd jobs that fell upon adjutants in the German navy.

The weeks rolled by as Rogge kept at his task. He brought in Korvettenkapitän Lorenzen, who outranked him, in theory at least, and was also the owner of a textile factory. Lorenzen was administrative officer. A man who could run a factory ought to be able to run the administrative problems of a ship, even a raider. Rogge pulled wires extending even to Berlin to secure the appointment of Dr. Reil as Marine-Stabsarzt, or chief surgeon, for the doctor had served under him on two training ships and he found this particular surgeon's abilities to extend far beyond the medical. He looked over others and chose as assistant surgeon a young Dr. Sprung and a weather officer, Dr. Collmann.

Then came the question of selecting a crew, and where another might have left this to his adjutant and the administrative officer, Captain Rogge did not. He took a look at what the personnel office had sent him as crew and simply exploded.

"Headquarters seemed to have been under the impression that they could unload on me all their riff-raff—men under punishment, confirmed idlers, anyone who had proved to be unemployable elsewhere," he wrote later.

Not so, headquarters soon found.

The commandant called the men before him one at a time and began asking questions. . . .

Here was a typical interview:

NAME?
Seaman So-and-So.
HOW MANY YEARS' SERVICE?
Four, Herr Kapitän.
WHY WEREN'T YOU PROMOTED?
I didn't agree with my captain.
THANK YOU, MOVE TO THE LEFT.

Movement to the left meant the men would be sent back to the marine barracks; those who were told to stand to the right would stay with the ship. Of 214 men sent in the original draft Rogge returned 104, coolly demanded a new draft, and specified a dozen men he wanted from his old training ship *Albert Leo Schlageter*. To secure transfer of men from the Baltic command to the North Sea command, also transfer of men from a going ship to a mystery mission, was not a simple operation— as if an American commander in Norfolk blithely asked for a dozen men from the Mare Island naval yard by name. It was a measure of Rogge's intentness on his mission that within a matter of days he had his dozen men from the training ship, and the new draft of reasonably effective seamen. He wanted a handpicked crew because he knew the job ahead. He knew the job ahead because he worked at discovering it almost twenty hours a day.

The *Goldenfels*, which now became *Ship 16*, was 500 feet long and 60 feet in the beam. She drew 25 feet of water, and in a pinch could manage 17.5 knots. She went into dry dock for conversion—but nobody was quite sure what they were converting her to. The Weser Company tried to find out, but there were absolutely no plans in existence for a prototype of a raider. All that had been learned in World War I was locked up in the brains of the men who had sailed those ships across the seas.

So to find out what he must know, Captain Rogge twice went to visit Fregattenkapitän Nerger, who had commanded the old raider *Wolf* in World War I, setting a record of 450 days at sea in the Atlantic and Indian Oceans. From Nerger he learned the

facts of life: the need for camouflage materials, the proper way
of opening the flaps of the artificial bulkheads which hid the
guns of the raider. He secured many other tips which were to
serve him well in the months to come.

Rogge was almost everywhere. He went to Hamburg to meet
with captains of other ships designated as raiders and to
exchange plans and information. He went to Berlin for briefing
by naval staffmen. He came back to the dockyard to see how
the ship was coming along, and to hear reports of the scrounging
activities of Kapitänleutnant Kühn. In this department, Kühn was
undoubtedly one of the presiding geniuses of German naval
affairs. He served in the navy for thirty years, boy and man,
enlisted man and officer. He knew where most ship's stores ever
unloaded might be found. From one port to another, from one
dockyard to the next, he sent raiding parties which came back
with the materials *Ship 16* was going to need.

It was very well that this was so. The adjutant, Leutnant zur
See Dr. Ulrich Mohr, reserve officer and chemist, was having
a miserable time working through channels. Take the matter of
flare pistols: he wanted four of them. Not a very expensive item,
not a very rare one. But after fourteen telephone calls to
headquarters he still did not have them because some staff officer
could not understand why *Ship 16* might need something that
was not listed on the official manifest. Mohr telephoned Berlin.
He called the Admiralty. He called Wilhelmshaven, the Baltic
command, and the admiral in command of naval dockyards.
Each office referred him to another or said the matter would be
considered. Finally, when Rogge came back from one of his
trips, he sent a report on the situation to Grand Admiral
Raeder—and then *Ship 16* got the four flare pistols she might
very well need if she took a prize.

The days crept by. Mohr fought the chairborne admirals for
five hundred books for the ship's library. Rogge fought dock
officials to secure the housing accommodations he wanted for
officers and men. He wanted each man to live close to his action
station, and each to have a bunk if possible (this was not
possible, as it turned out). Every officer had a cabin, and the
chief petty officers were berthed in single or double cabins, petty
officers in fours and eights, and enlisted men in messes of
eighteen to fifty men.

The Admiralty had not been totally blind to the possibility of war when *Goldenfels* was built, and a special secret naval subsidy had made it possible for her owners to construct the decks to accommodate reinforcements on which 150 mm. guns could be mounted. But that was about the only difference between *Goldenfels* and any other merchantman of her period. In the confusions and hurries of the first weeks of war, it took the dockyard fourteen weeks to outfit the ship. Outfitting meant many things, from choosing pictures for the wardroom wall (no pinups but a painting by Franz Marc called "The Red Horses") to flowers in the seamen's quarters.

Fourteen long weeks—and even that miracle was accomplished only because Captain Rogge spent many an hour over glasses of beer and schnapps with the yard engineers. No one had expected *Ship 16* to be first out of the yards, but she was months ahead of the others of her class.

Four-fifths of the crew was mustered and aboard by early December when the guns began going into place, the arms that made the men feel for the first time that they were aboard a ship of war. She was to carry six 150 mm. guns, with a 75 mm. warning gun in the bow to shoot across the bows of merchantmen and bring them up short in time-honored commerce raider fashion. But there was armament aboard the new raider that had never been heard of in *Wolf* and *Moewe* and *Seeadler* and the rest: she carried two twin 37 mm. anti-aircraft guns, and four 20 mm. automatic guns, *and* two seaplanes of her own, HE 114's. In addition, she had torpedo tubes amidships on either side at the waterline, and a compartment for mines that was capable of stowing 92 magnetic mines.

Like a good captain, Rogge was never satisfied. He wanted more. Particularly since he was going to be gone so far from his homeland on this voyage to harry enemy shipping, he finally wanted another airplane for spotting purposes. The request was turned down, and like the good captain he was, he shrugged his shoulders and forgot it. He had done his best. He could do no more.

CHAPTER FOUR

Raider 16

On December 19, 1939, the German Admiralty commissioned a new warship, *Ship 16—Raider 16*—which was to be known to Captain Rogge and his men as *Atlantis* and to the British, when they discovered her, as *Raider C*. The crew continued to pour aboard until it consisted of the complete quota of 21 officers and 328 men under Rogge, who was advanced in rank to Kapitän zur See, the four-stripe captaincy of navies the world over.

Raider 16 sat in harbor at Bremen through the Christmas season, trying out little by little. She went out into the Weser River to try out her various camouflage equipment—what Rogge indulgently called "the gadgets." The men began accustoming themselves to life aboard this ship, and on December 28 they set out for Kiel to take on stores and ammunition at the naval yard. Being in inland waters, Captain Rogge turned the conn over to a professional river pilot, and they had scarcely begun to clear port when the pilot ran the ship aground.

Leutnant Fehler, the demolition expert, was undaunted.

"What are you all worrying about," he said cheerfully to the dismayed officers on the bridge. "It's a good omen. Don't you remember that *Wolf* went aground at the start, and look at what a wonderful career she had!"

Captain Kamenz, the old seadog and navigator, snarled him down.

"*Ja*, imbecile," he said, "and look what happened to her captain!"

It was true, of course, that the omen was not necessarily so good, based on the *Wolf* case. For in World War I, when *Wolf*

14

had been run aground by her captain in the Elbe at the beginning of her voyage, the admirals in Berlin and Wilhelmshaven had not taken the action kindly. The commander of *Wolf* was arbitrarily dismissed in favor of Fregattenkapitän Nerger. It was not enough for the captain of a raider to have "skill," the Admiralty said in dismissing the first captain—although again a pilot had been at fault—a raider captain must also have *luck*.

Raider 16 sat for six hours in the mud of the Weser, her officers worrying what the Admiralty might do if the Führer found out what had happened to her. But if the Admiralty knew of the new ship's misfortune, the news was never transmitted to Hitler's headquarters, and no official cognizance was taken of the unfortunate affair. On January 31, at Kiel, the officers and crew were signally honored by an inspection visit from no less a personage than Grand Admiral Raeder himself.

After he had been piped aboard, the admiral walked about the ship briskly, his firm jaw jutting and his sharp eyes darting everywhere. "Most excellently equipped," he said, when he had completed the inspection. And he did not mention at all the unfortunate incident of the grounding in the Weser.

Then the grand day was over. The task was to make ready for sea, and wait for the Admiralty's pleasure in sailing.

In January and February the crew practiced their changes on the ship, using the camouflage material to make her into "different ships," one after another. A dummy funnel could be set up. The real funnel could be lengthened or shortened to create different silhouettes. The masts were tripods which moved up and down at will. The ship even had dummy guns, to simulate an armed merchantman or even a minesweeper. The real guns were concealed in huge crates that were labeled to indicate deck cargo.

In those weeks the crew became adept at changing the form of the raider, and meanwhile Captain Rogge studied his Admiralty orders until he knew them by heart.

His chief task was to divert enemy naval forces from their home waters and to inflict damage on the enemy in any way he could. That task was the time-honored duty of the merchant raider; it had not varied since the Hundred Years' War. The tactics, however, were quite different in this modern day. Rogge's success would lie in the ship's ability to create enough furor that the English would have to form convoys and allocate capital ships to duty in remote waters of the world. The English would have to use their naval forces heavily in search of the raiders, thus freeing the submarines and taking pressure off German waters. The raiders would frighten neutral shipping by their activity and would thus help starve England into submission.

The Admiralty had also refined the raider technique since the days of *Wolf* and *Moewe:* these ships had gone out to sink as many enemy vessels as possible in as short a time as possible and generally create havoc. The new technique called for the raider simply to survive, to be a "raider in being," and by its continued existence to keep the enemy preoccupied and alert with the least possible danger to the ship itself.

Surprise, then, was the order of the day, surprise upon surprise that would force the English navy to send her cruisers out to protect trade. "This will ease the situation on the home front and will slow down the enemy's overseas trade considerably owing to the need for escorts," said the orders from Seekriegsleitung—SKL—the operational staff of the naval high command.

The disguises, said the orders, would be used continually to change the appearance of the ship, thus increasing surprise and confusing the British as to the number and nature of raiders in any given region of the world. A raider would operate in a single area just as long as possible. Then, when the enemy had learned of the raider's existence and nature, she was to leave that area and move to an area far enough away that whatever protective enemy moves had been made would not be effective in this new location. But, by the same token, the raider must stay in her first area long enough for the enemy to be forced to take some defensive measure. One of the great values of the raiders was to keep the British navy constantly off balance by forcing them to set up one defense, only to discover that the raider against whom they were defending was gone and was operating successfully somewhere else in the world.

Also, the captain must be ready and able to make his cruiser disappear totally in remote areas, so that whatever the means of tracking her down, the enemy would be thrown off the scent.

Rogge was to avoid actions with enemy forces, including auxiliary cruisers if possible: the Germans recalled too well how their raiders had been overcome many times in World War I by superior British auxiliaries. Further, the Germans were to leave convoys alone and avoid passenger ships, which would probably be superior in speed, and might even be superior in armament to the raider. In any event, if *Raider 16* captured a passenger vessel, the crew and passengers would embarrass her considerably.

World War I's surface raiders had been notable for their restraint in management of attacked vessels: that is, most captains had been careful to observe accepted international procedure in fighting their sea war. They had overhauled the enemy or suspected merchantman, had put a shot across her bow, brought her to "heave to" and await a boarding party. Then the boarding party had gone across the water and inspected the other ship's papers. If the ship was a neutral, even one carrying a noncontraband cargo to an enemy nation, she would be freed. If she was an enemy vessel, her crew would be put aboard the raider, and she would be sunk or taken as a prize to be sent home or to a neutral port. She might, in a case where a raider had sunk several ships and captured many men, be used as a barracks ship for transport of all the assembled prisoners to a neutral port. Or those prisoners might be put aboard a neutral ship stopped specifically for that purpose.

That was all in World War I. Even in the later years of that war, technical changes in naval warfare interfered with the time- and nation-honored practices of gentlemanly conduct in behalf of human life. More and more ships were equipped with radio each year during that war, and radio meant that the captains were under order to signal their course and position when attacked by a raider. Nothing could be done to save the vessel attacked, in all probability, but the raider might be tracked down thus, and certainly she would be forced to move about rapidly, thus decreasing her own usefulness.

By World War II's beginning, odd was the ship that did not have radio. Only a handful of tramp vessels of very ancient vintage would be without modern communications, which meant weather information, shipping information, and conveniences of many kinds during peacetime. But war—what general use of radio meant would not be quite comprehended by anyone on the eve of the war. For Germany, SKL reserved the right to make the decisions regarding the rules of warfare. Rogge was told to follow international treaties and conventions as far as possible.

But what that meant was completely changed by the following orders:

> As, however, the war has to be waged in such a way as best to further the war effort as a whole, it goes without saying that the employment of effective weapons and of certain tactics cannot fall away because one or other international rule or regulation is against it. The political repercussions of measures which go beyond the accepted law can be appreciated and judged only by SKL: for this reason SKL reserves to itself the right to order the carrying out of such measures.

So Captain Rogge and those who would come after him were to go to sea, fight the war as they saw fit under their regulations as long as SKL approved. But the final judgment as to how they would fight was retained, headquarters said, in its own hands.

It promised to become a difficult situation.

CHAPTER FIVE

World War II: Early 1940

Captain Rogge had hoped to leave German waters in November or December, and take advantage of the long winter night in the north to make the breakthrough, up the coast of Norway, across the dangerous waters far north of Iceland, down along the Greenland coast to mid-Atlantic, and then south to begin his work in the southern oceans. But there were delays in the beginning, in the outfitting at Kiel, and then the winter of 1939–40 turned out to be one of the cold ones, when the North Sea froze over early and hard. *Raider 16* (*Atlantis*) sat at dockside in Kiel masquerading as a depot ship, painted naval gray, wearing heavy naval searchlights on her crossbeams and her crew in uniform as they chipped ice in the rigging and on the decks nearly every day.

They had in their possession a keepsake, a de luxe edition of the operational orders drawn up for the raiders, bound in red morocco with deep gold block and marked thoughtfully: YOU WILL NEVER SURRENDER.

Never surrender? Captain Rogge and his crew wondered if they were ever going to fight.

They knew, by February, that they were somehow caught up in the logjam of Admiralty planning. What they did not know was that the German naval strategy was in the process of complete change, and that they were simply victims of circumstance, victimized as much as anything else because nobody had time to think about them.

The German navy, having been promised so much—and especially time—by Adolf Hitler, found itself in the fall of 1939 part way along in a ship-building program that it could never

19

hope to complete. The navy was building battleships, cruisers, and aircraft carriers, and it was quickly apparent that what was needed was submarines. Admiral Doenitz had hoped to send surface forces out to challenge British might in the North Sea, but this was impossible. As for British defense, it was quickly aroused, including defense against raiders; and in October, 1939, no fewer than eight raider-hunting forces were set loose by the Allies. In December, the commerce-raiding warship *Graf Spee* was brought to naval action and then trapped in the Plate River of South America. *Deutschland*, another pocket battleship, made her way back to Kiel after doing a minimum of damage to shipping.

In this period of the war, the German naval staff accepted the theory that the primary need of German operations was to attack British sea communications. Why not get *Raider 16* into action then, along with her sisters?

Two problems presented themselves: one was the absolute insistence that the raiders be secure against identification—and against the new weapon that had been perfected since World War I, the observing airplane. Second was the gap between theory and performance. The naval staff knew what to do but it was not being done quickly. One reason was the growing German preoccupation with Norway, a preoccupation which held the navy in its grip. In the 1920's Vice Admiral Wolfgang Wegener had written a study of naval strategy in World War I which showed how greater use of Norwegian waters might have changed the course of the sea war. So there was pressure from the navy to take over Norway. In December, 1939, Hitler was convinced that Norway must be occupied. And so, in the early months of 1940 when, by Captain Rogge's standards, a great deal of attention should have been given the problems of the commerce raiders that were trying to get to sea, naval headquarters was concerning itself with a whole new set of plans involving the navy's part in the Norwegian invasion.

The ship was ready. The officers and crew were ready, over-trained if anything, and burning with eagerness to get out of the frozen north and into the tropical waters where they would operate. Theoretically they were maintaining security. When lighters were brought alongside with munitions, First Officer Kühn waited carefully until the tugs were well away from the scene before beginning the loading. It would not do to have talk:

a depot ship did not carry large quantities of torpedoes, 150 mm., 75 mm., 37 mm., and 20 mm. ammunition.

There were still difficulties in getting everything needed, as there had been from the beginning. They found it almost impossible to secure a bubble sextant for navigation, and they never did get the up-to-date fire control equipment they wanted, because the Admiralty said it simply wasn't worth the risk; the equipment was in short supply and *Raider 16*'s degree of expendability was too great: they might be sunk before they had a chance to use the fire control gear, said SKL.

So March began, a blustery chilling March that few who had lived in the North Sea region would soon forget; the Kiel Canal was frozen tight.

In the second week of March all was ready; so, apparently, was Berlin ready to let the raiders go. Captain Rogge saw to it that everything was made shipshape, and that plans were carried out for the Easter leaves which were coming up very soon. He asked the Kiel naval base for two targets and two ships to be made available for firing practice off Pilau after Easter. Then he left for Berlin and what he knew was his final briefing session with the Admiralty.

He returned from Berlin on March 12, and told Kühn to get the ship under way. There was a problem of discipline which had arisen in his absence: a man had flatly refused to obey an order. Rogge would countenance many breaches of the German naval regulations by a loyal and disciplined crew that he could trust, but he could not and would not trust a man who would not obey orders. The seaman was given new orders—to get his duffel together—and was landed on the pier while a work detail headed for the naval barracks and took a man to replace him then and there. Half an hour later, the naval depot ship began moving out to the Elbe estuary, flags flying in the cold wind, twin funnels overhead so artfully disguised, and guns trained fore and aft as regulations provided.

Raider 16, chameleon of the sea, was setting out on her long voyage.

CHAPTER SIX

Into Action

Slowly, her propellers chewing up the broken ice behind her in the channel, the grim, gray depot ship headed for the Holtenau Lock behind the target ship *Hessen*, which was breaking ice. Two days were spent in company with Captain Weyher in *Raider 36* and Captain von Ruckteschell in *Raider 21*, now camouflaged as Boom defense vessels, just in case some nosy British aircraft might be about. Of the many classes of ships deemed fair game, minesweepers were generally of little interest, so specialized their task and so apparently inoffensive were they.

Until this time, *Raider 16* had been bothered by the cold in carrying out her gunnery qualification program before sailing into action. Along with *Raider 36*, this task was now completed in a few days, and the ship was ready to proceed. On March 24 she lay anchored off Suederpiep, disguised now as the Norwegian freighter *Knute Nelson*, with green hull, white superstructure, and flying a yellow quarantine flag. She also sported, courtesy of the expert camouflage artists, a handsome single funnel. All this had been accomplished in the cold night of March 23, by shaded light. The crewmen had been haled up from their warm bunks and messrooms, to swing from cradles around the hull or scamper up the masts. And the security measures were not confined to the ship: they had left in Kiel a trusted officer, who was stacking up the mail. One man had been left behind with the specific task of going every day to the fleet post office to collect mail for the ship *Atlantis*, the so-called depot ship. He would go in the morning, pick up the bags, bring them back to this secret storeroom, and sort them out. In a few days a small mountain of mail collected for the men of the depot ship—mail they would not see for years, if ever. Rogge was taking as few chances as he might on a slip-up to the British agents that might be anywhere.

It was almost time for the breakout, the attempt to run the very effective British blockade. The Germans and British together had laid a huge series of minefields which extended down into the North Sea like a great U, that ran down the Scottish coast, flattened off the German shore, and ran up the Norwegian coast to a point off the Orkneys. The British had also mined heavily all the waters between the northern coast of Scotland and Iceland! Here the old escape channel was no longer usable—the Germans must travel north around Iceland to be safe from the dreaded minefields; and so effective were the mines that the British navy had far less territory to watch than had the navy of World War I. Getting through—breaking out—had not been easy in the first war, and a number of German warships had fallen prey to the blockaders. But comparatively, the task of breakout in World War II was several times as difficult, and all depended on absolute security and behavior that would have seemed totally farfetched thirty years before.

The planning had been very detailed and very careful—at least on the part of Captain Rogge and the members of the crew of *Raider 16*. The captain, after thinking it over, had decided to break out disguised as a Russian merchantman.

His reasoning was precise:

"The ports of the Soviet are free of prying eyes," he told his crew, so the British would not be likely to know the whereabouts of any Russian ship in the register. Or there could be Russian ships not in the register at all. Then there was the language barrier. Anyone with a rudimentary knowledge of Russian could fool the average British investigator in this regard. It simply took a few words in the Cyrillic alphabet, a few signs that were unmistakably Russian, and a tremendous amount of gall to pull it off.

In these early months of the war, the Soviet Union was neutral. More than that, Russian officials were cultivating the German foreign office furiously, trying to buy time for the Russian military machine to be built up, some officials hoping even that the Russians and the Germans would not go to war. The Germans, for their part, were not eager to stir up any trouble at all with the Russians. When Captain Rogge's plan to escape detection by posing as a Russian freighter was announced at the Admiralty, it was received with mixed emotions. Undoubtedly, admitted all, there was much to be said for Rogge's reasoning, but the politics of the action were something else again.

Rogge made the matter official by asking Berlin to find him a Soviet naval ensign that he might fly as he broke through the blockade. It was promised, but to be delivered only in a plain wrapper and directly to Rogge, in the most complete secrecy.

The flag was delivered: it came by ordinary mail. It was addressed to the chief of staff at Wilhelmshaven, it was opened by inspectors, and opened again by the chief of staff's office, and the chief himself asked why Rogge was collecting Russian flags. If there was a British spy within the camp, his ears would have begun wiggling. But no spy had apparently infiltrated the Kiel base and so the flag was delivered and stowed away without incident.

The green-funneled "Norwegian" lay off Suederpiep on the Schleswig-Holstein coast for several days, and the weather grew worse and worse. One night just before the end of the month, the men of magic with their camouflage plans came out again from the cabins and messrooms of the ship and in the fog that shrouded their ship they changed her again, from Norwegian freighter to Russian Fleet Auxiliary Cruiser *Kim*. She wore a hammer and sickle on her bridge, a great red star on No. 2 hatch and over her counter the inscription:

ОСТЕРЕГАЙТЕС ВНHT

which in plain English meant "keep clear of the propellers." But whatever it meant in plain English would be undecipherable to a plain Englishman, and that was precisely the effect intended.

In the dirty weather of the last day of March, *Raider 16* set sail as the Russian ship *Kim*. She was accompanied by two torpedo boats who stayed with her until evening, several alternating flights of Messerschmitt fighters and Heinkel 115's for air cover, and trailing her a U-boat, which was to escort her as far as the Denmark Strait.

The way they looked and the way they wanted to look was as a Russian ship that had been visiting Germany and was heading homeward. The way they were going and what they were in fact doing was moving steadily northward to the Bergen-Shetlands route between western Norway and the island group north of Scotland.

Sailing came in conditions unusual for the North Sea in early spring. The wind varied between south and southwest, the skies were overcast and muddy, the sea was heavy and rising, and the wind was coming up, which with rising sea and cloud cover cut visibility to five miles, and the temperature was hovering around zero. In a word, when asked about the weather, the captain called it filthy.

The first day passed uneventfully. Earlier, in port, they had been overflown by British scouting planes, but the British had seen the Norwegian freighter riding at quarantine—they had not yet noted the neutral Russian warship heading "home." The first night fell, black and evil, just the way Captain Rogge wanted it, with visibility near the zero point. He had a word for such weather: *Durchbruchswetter*, or breakout weather. The wind might howl in their ears, and the cold snap at their noses and mittened hands, and the spray might rise to the top of the funnel and break over the crosstrees of the masts, but this was just what the captain would have ordered. The problem was to achieve that first danger point safely: the narrows between western Norway and the Shetlands.

It was wind, rain, and spray all night long. Below was warm enough, but let a man step out onto the bridge and his hands froze and his eyes watered in the cold while the spattering rain tore at his ears and stiffened his hair against the foul weather gear.

All night long the captain and his officers were on the lookout for what they dreaded: the British cruisers reported operating in the narrows region. But they saw nothing. Dawn brought more of the same weather, and no Britishers. The ship plunged along at high speed on her course, the U-boat making heavy weather behind her, but managing.

Toward evening, the men of *Raider 16* sighted three fishing boats off the Klondyke Bank. They might be fishing boats; they might be naval spotters for the British, too, but that was simply a chance *Raider 16* would have to take, trusting to her disguise to pull her through. Captain Rogge stuck to his course and speed. The U-boat—*U-37*—kept taking the pounding, too.

Not long afterward, the radio operator reported that he was receiving five-letter code groups on several frequencies. The British naval code was sent in four-or-five-letter groups. Did that mean the fishing boats were not what they seemed to be, and that they were reporting to the cruisers over the horizon somewhere, or that the air service had earlier reported on the Bergen line?

As night fell, the wind swung around the compass, from south to northeast and then north, and with the cold wind came the storm, which rose to Force 8, and began kicking up the seas. The ship and its submarine escort still must plow through to pass the dangerous narrows.

There had been three dangers: the channel through the minefields; the Neck, which they were now approaching; and the Denmark Strait, which was the entrance to the North Atlantic. They had passed the gap in the first hours, and one danger was behind them. They could hear the British cruisers they feared so much, and those cruisers patrolled the Neck they were approaching. Then would come the Strait, where British aircraft moved out from the Shetlands in any kind of flying weather, and where British auxiliary cruisers roamed in nearly all weather.

This night of April 5–6 as the ship plunged through the heavy seas, straining and shuddering in the blows she took as she headed straight into the wind, U-37 finally gave up the fight. She could no longer keep up surface speed heading into those monster waves; her commander feared that she might spring a leak or that his crew might be hurt in the battering. So it was agreed that U-37 should leave them—what good could she do for protection on a night like this when visibility was nearly zero and the pitching and tossing seas would make it impossible to take and hold a firing position? U-37 dropped back with an *Auf wiedersehn* and a promise to meet the raider east of Denmark Strait.

The night continued foul, the wind shifting to north-northwest and growing stronger; the spray rose as high as the top of the funnel—indeed, it was a night for breakout if there ever was one.

In the gray of dawn the lookouts made out the upper works of two ships, one carrying navigation lights and the other blacked out. Rogge had a new intelligence report which showed three British cruisers operating in the narrow area called the Neck, and three British auxiliaries working the Denmark Strait.

It would be a close shave.

As Rogge watched, and the guns were manned and all the men came to action stations, the ships turned toward *Raider 16*, and he could see the black smudge of smoke forming behind the funnel of the first ship. A red light showed on the foremast of the leading ship, and Rogge knew it was not a navigation light. It might be the light of a command unit, which meant warships and, since there were no German warships operating in this area, unfriendly warships.

The captain looked his approval at the way Gunnery Officer Kasch had put his men into their paces—the first alert of the voyage. He called Chief Engineer Kielhorn to the bridge and asked how much speed he might expect.

The answer was 16 or 17 knots. He asked the chief to do his best, and the roundfaced Bavarian went below, and there pushed the engines to produce 17.5 knots. *Raider 16* began to surge forward in rushes, moving ahead bow up on the crest of a wave, and stern plunging into the trough behind, shuddering and shaking until the men's teeth clacked, the plates shrieking and bending and all unsecured small items rolling and tossing around below.

It was no way to treat a ship in a storm, urging her to top speed—but Rogge had the hunch that if he did not escape these following masts, it would make no difference whether or not *Raider 16* was able to withstand such a gale. So on they went, clanking and shuddering in the icy spray for hours, until the mastheads of the other ships disappeared below the horizon. Then, the moment he was sure he had evaded what he knew to be enemies, Captain Rogge telegraphed the engine room to reduce speed, and the shaking stopped as the ship settled down to work her way moderately in the wind and waves.

By eleven o'clock on the morning of April 6 the ship had turned northeast and headed into the storm at its highest point—gale strength. An hour later, 624 miles out from port, the raider was in the danger zone, the neck of the Bergen-Shetlands shipping route, and vile as the weather appeared to every man in the crew, Captain Rogge was thankful for it. For a good seaman in a stout ship could brave the rigors of the sea, and

those dangers in such waters were to be preferred to the charging
of the huntsmen who were searching that day for such as he.

Heading in the direction of Murmansk as they were, the
Germans hoped to fool their enemies. The chance came soon
for Rogge: they saw a Wilhelmsen Company freighter, the
Taronga, but gave her a wide berth and she paid them little
attention. On deck, in addition to the other marks that identified
the raider as Russian, was riding one of their aircraft wearing
distinctive Russian marking—and perhaps that was the clincher.

In any event, *Taronga* passed them by without a word spoken
either to them or through the ether to British naval headquarters.
Not long afterward, the lookouts sang out:

"*Schiff in Sicht!*"

This time it was a pair of tall masts, approaching from so
unusual an angle that Rogge knew they could not be those of a
normal freighter traveling on the normal lane. So, of course, he
suspected that the other was an armed auxiliary. On the bridge
the officers focused their binoculars and waited. The ship
approached, then turned and made off at full speed.

Speak of the luck of the raiders? Rogge had it.

CHAPTER SEVEN

Breakthrough

Captain Rogge did not know it, but he was very near to being caught up in the midst of the battle for control of Norway. On the last day of March, the British cruiser *Birmingham* and two destroyers were sent out from Scapa Flow to capture enemy fishing vessels and cover the forces that were to lay mines in Norwegian waters. Earlier, *Raider 16* had come close enough alongside some mines to identify them as English in origin. Three separate British forces were operating in the area, no fewer than fifteen ships being scheduled to be off the Norwegian coast on April 5. Fortunately for Rogge's chances, the British Admiralty advanced the date for this Operation Wilfred—but the waters between England and Norway were virtually swarming with British ships in these last few days before what turned out to be the German invasion of Norway. *Raider 16* was moving rapidly northeast, however, which meant away from the action. There were still some tense moments—an airplane appeared off the coast and circled. The men were called to action stations again, and the binoculars raised and lowered, but the plane was identified as a Dornier 26, a slow, effective flying boat, but a German, and then it swung away and was gone.

Soon the storm died down, to a north-northwest breeze with moderate northeast swell, and as darkness fell the skies were streaked with brilliant fan-shaped rays of light—the northern lights, and green St. Elmo's fire—which had also greeted the raiders of *Moewe* and other German ships in the war fought more than a quarter of a century earlier.

By the morning of April 8 the ship crossed the Arctic Circle, still pretending to head for Murmansk, still unwatched and

unopposed. It would not be long now before she would make a
sharp turn westward, and move onto the Murmansk-Iceland
route. They were moving to a point identified by the submarine
commander as Point Nixe, off Jan Mayen Island, where *U-37*
was to join them and resume the escort until the breakthrough
was achieved. At that point, ice conditions permitting, the ship
and submarine would move north to pass around Iceland.
Conditions not permitting, they would head south of the big
island, hoping to avoid British minefields and the cruisers they
expected to see in those waters. By evening the turn was made,
another commitment to the breakthrough, and the ship headed
into the wind and storm-tossed sea once more.

Now they need only pass their last hazard, the Denmark
Strait, and they would be in the Atlantic, having accomplished
what the Germans called *Durchbruch*, the breakthrough. To
Rogge and the men of *Raider 16* it meant escape and challenge.
They were heading steadily toward the point where they would
succeed or fail.

Toward evening of the next day, *Raider 16* approached Jan
Mayen Island. All day long the weather had been clearing, off
the island there was no wind at all, and the sea glimmered like
a gray mirror. Off the island was the submarine, which had been
waiting for hours at the rendezvous point. She refueled from the
raider (one of Rogge's duties was to act as depot ship for
submarines).

While they waited, the submarine commander and Rogge
discussed the ice situation. Neither had an up-to-date weather
forecast or report on ice conditions, and of course, the only way
they could be secured was by submarine observation in the area.
Had there been enough time and had the ships assigned to the
work done their job? Rogge believed not. He wanted to attempt
the Denmark Strait, but he suspected that the pack would be
frozen and that he and the submarine would be forced to move
south into the more dangerous waters. Yet the raider's luck held
again, for even as they waited, a meteorological report came in
telling them that the ice conditions in the Strait were good
enough at that moment to permit passage north of the island.

So the fueling was finished and the ship and surfaced U-boat
headed into Denmark Strait, loafing along during the afternoon
so they might make the passage by night.

As night fell and they moved northwest, the wind rose, and

the ice floes came in view during the first dogwatch. In two hours, by measurement, the temperature of the water dropped from 33°F. to 27°F. Shortly after midnight the ice became thicker and Rogge headed south—and conditions grew worse. By dawn, the U-boat was so heavily iced that she reported she could not crash-dive in case of emergency. The water was at the freezing point and was gray and murky, and the air temperature was 19° below zero!

U-boat and raider continued to move along together toward the line of the northern ice pack. As if the cold was not enough, they were in storm again. The seas poured across the decks, freezing in sheets and stacking up ice everywhere there was a protuberance. Up the bow plunged, and then down, through mountainous waves that rolled across the hatch tops and down the companionways. Worst was the icing of the guns, for the ship must be kept in fighting trim, so the men hacked at the ice on the mounts with picks and shovels and burned it off the guns with torches, only to find that minutes later it had formed again.

The U-boat took a far worse beating, and when she could be seen at all she was a silvery fish moving in and out of the waves. The U-boat captain had indicated his willingness to go as far as the barrier, which meant to 67° 24' North, and 24° West. By the time they achieved that position, the submarine was so badly iced up that she was no longer capable of action and was in danger of flooding through the conning tower hatch, which had frozen in a partly open condition. A really bad sea might sink her. So *U-37* heaved to, while *Raider 16* stood by watching anxiously. And then the raider went on without its protection, plowing through a southeasterly gale.

For hours the raider plowed through freezing waters, heading west. There was little if any danger from enemy shipping here, but there was plenty of danger from icebergs which tore loose and pushed into the Atlantic. Just after midnight of April 7, however, the ship entered the Gulf Stream, and in a matter of hours the water temperature rose from freezing to 42°. By eight o'clock in the morning, the ship was off Cape Farewell at the southern tip of Greenland and was heading south. The *Durchbruch* had been successful.

CHAPTER EIGHT

We Are Japanese,
If You Please

The plans for *Raider 16* that had been worked out in Berlin called for her to refrain from attacking any ships until she reached the trade route that ran between Freetown and the Cape of Good Hope. But after the breakthrough of April 7, events moved rapidly in Europe and changed those plans considerably. The German invasion of Norway occurred on April 9. Next day a British destroyer flotilla moved into Narvik and shot up five German destroyers lying in harbor there, disabling three of them, then engaging five more German destroyers anchored in a fjord off the port. This fierce fight was followed by other naval attacks and British air attacks until Supreme Headquarters in Berlin began to grow nervous. Six of the first seven cargo ships sent to support the invasion were sunk by the British. British submarines moved back and forth, creating havoc. And so, on April 16, headquarters sent out an urgent radio message changing the orders of *Raider 16* and of *Raider 36*, which had followed *Raider 16* out. They were to get into action, begin sinking as many British ships as possible, and call attention to their presence in the Atlantic to divert British naval forces from Norway.

Captain Rogge was not particularly pleased with this change of orders, which endangered his mission and probably would do very little good to the forces in Norway in any case. So he compromised: he would begin sinking ships but he would do everything possible to keep them from sending off radio messages. (Radio messages were just what the German Admiralty wanted at that moment.)

Raider 16 steamed south at a steady 10 knots, using only one engine.

The ship crossed the Atlantic shipping lanes in no time. As she moved south, the cold weather gear of the men was changed for summer white, and the heading was set for 12° South, 2° West, a point about halfway between Ascension and St. Helena islands, which would put them on the Cape Town-Freetown shipping lane where they intended to operate for a time.

Raider 16 was still "Russian." The topmasts were brought down one step and the crow's nests were removed, for no ordinary merchant ship would be so equipped, and to keep them up was to advertise the raider's business to the world. When the seas calmed and the weather warmed, Captain Rogge took the cutter out one day and moved slowly around his ship, making sure that she appeared to be a merchantman. She had taken some pounding in the breakout, and some of her Russian insignia had washed away, but she still looked the part of a merchant ship, and that was what mattered.

As the weather warmed the men again went into practice for their corsair's work. So effective had been the plans worked out in the Bremen dockyard that the men could be called to action stations and the heavy guns run out for firing in a matter of seconds!

On April 22 *Raider 16* crossed the equator, and continued to move south, now aided by radio reports based on British documents captured in Norway which gave details about enemy sea routes and convoys. Captain Rogge was still trying to avoid detection until he reached his most favored position, so when they approached two different ships, they gave them both broad berth and the others moved on. Next day, Captain Rogge ordered the engines stopped, and the men went over the side on rope-rigged stages to repaint the huge spots on the hull which had been stripped bare by wind and ice. The duty watch worked in the warm sun, while the off-duty watch looked on, cracking jokes, lazing in the sun, and fishing for sharks in these tropical waters.

Before the serious business of war began, there was a bit of time for some tomfoolery, and it came on April 24, when Admiral Triton came aboard the ship to preside over the ceremonies of "crossing the line" and inducting 250 new "shellbacks" into the mysteries of the Kingdom of Neptune. Along with Triton appeared his guard of honor, seamen equipped with stiff deck brooms as arms, dressed in their "skivvies," and wearing foul weather hats and rubber boots. Grass skirts were broken out for the "princesses" and warriors. Liberal quantities of fuel oil were smeared across the faces and backs of the "pollywogs" (*sonderfall*), and "doctors" wearing phony spectacles, straw hats, and false beards scampered about the decks "treating" patients who were unlucky enough to come under their care.

Neptune, in a blond wig and beard, presided over all along with the captain, who wore a huge medallion. The initiates were barbered and thrown into the ship's swimming pool, smacked with paddles, and given noxious food and drink. Then, when all the initiates were cleansed of their sins and the dust of the northern hemisphere, and the fuel oil was somewhat washed off, there was coffee and cake and beer for the crew, and an afternoon of freedom for most of them.

Now it was time to change disguise, for what would a Russian ship be doing in these southern waters? Oh, it was possible that a Russian might be that far out of her element, but so improbable that she was guaranteed to attract attention and this was precisely what Captain Rogge did not want until the proper moment.

Lieutenant Mohr, the adjutant, was the expert on camouflage, and he and Rogge got to work, even as the new "shellbacks" were below celebrating their exalted achievement. The Soviet ensign and the red stars were removed, a big K was painted on the funnel, and a flag of the Rising Sun broken out on the plating forward of the bridge and abaft the foremast, so she might be recognized as a neutral.

The Japanese disguise had not been chosen idly. For weeks before sailing, Mohr had been given the task of studying the ships that *Raider 16* might most easily impersonate. He had gone through thousands of names and descriptions in Lloyd's shipping register, looking for vessels of about 8,000 tons with cruiser sterns, which looked like *Raider 16*. Finally, he had narrowed the list to 26 ships which could possibly be used, and then had begun eliminating many of those. He had to cut out the ships that normally served African ports—for it would be most embarrassing to be pretending to be some ship and then run across the real thing with a British cruiser hanging around the vicinity. So the list of availables came down and down. Finally, Mohr settled on the *Kasii Maru* of the Kokusai Line, thus, the big K. There were many problems to be solved—most of them by First Officer Kühn—such as painting a waterline at the waterline while in the water; but by artificially canting the ship a bit this was accomplished and a sufficiently professional disguise was given *Raider 16*. She was now *Kasii Maru*, 8,408 tons, out of Tokyo, built in 1936, carrying radio call sign JHOJ. The hull was still black, the masts now yellowed, and the ventilators yellow outside and red inside, and funnel black with a red top and the big K. When all was finished, Rogge went out in his cutter again, circled the ship critically, and examined her through his glasses as well as by naked eye. He was pleased.

On April 28, Captain Rogge called the ship's company together and made a little speech. In a few days they would begin raiding, he said, but the crew was not to try to second-guess the captain. They would not take every ship they saw, but would follow their orders, which were to spread alarm among the enemy, force the British to use convoys in these waters, and destroy and delay enough shipping to hurt the British and the colonial economies.

The raider would also play the role of "fleet in being"—that is, she would attack and then disappear, and perhaps spend a long time in some inaccessible spot, simply to force the British to be on constant lookout for her, which meant the utilization of many British warships.

Nor would she look for trouble with British warships, or attack passenger vessels. The orders of SKL were now explained to the crew, it being Rogge's belief that if the crew knew generally what the ship was about, there would be less complaint and less questioning around the scuttlebutt.

On April 29, the disguise of the raider was complete. On the decks moved sailors wearing the white headscarves and outside blouses of the Japanese merchant navy. Some wore glasses. On the boat deck sat six "passengers," for the *Kasii Maru* was a combination freighter-passenger liner; and, to top it off, on the upper deck a Japanese "woman" pushed a baby carriage, as if she were out giving her baby a bit of air. How harmless, how neutral could a ship be?

Next day, April 30, the *Kasii Maru* reached the Cape Town-Freetown shipping lane, turned along it, and began her search. But almost immediately a gale blew up from east-southeast and sent the ship lunging through the waves, scud mast high. This was no weather for raiding.

May 1 brought nothing but messages from Germany describing general war situations and apparent British plans to divert shipping from the Mediterranean around the Cape of Good Hope. May 2 dawned with the lookouts straining for sight of a smoke cloud. Suddenly came the cry from the foremast:

"*Rauchwolke in Sicht!*" Smoke cloud in sight!

The crew of *Raider 16* sprang to action stations. Captain Rogge turned 40 degrees to port. The gunnery officer brought his men to a fine state of readiness at their guns. The "Japanese" appeared on deck in costume, and all others of the crew disappeared. Adjutant Mohr appeared on the bridge wearing a white kimono and straw hat over his navy blues.

"*Schornsteinkappe des Gegners ist heraus*"—Enemy funnel in sight—came the word from the masthead, and just then a call came to the bridge from the radio shack: a Belgian ship, the *Thysville*, was transmitting in this neighborhood.

The gray and black hull of a large passenger liner came up on the horizon very shortly and it was quickly apparent that she was not the *Thysville* but a passenger vessel armed with a 4.5-inch gun aft and anti-aircraft guns.

Captain Rogge watched her long and carefully through his glasses, and the men waited hopefully for the sign that they were going into action.

Finally the captain put down his binoculars.

"There will be no attack," he said.

The faces of his officers fell, and noting that disappointment, the captain explained: the ship passing probably carried 200 passengers and the raider was in no position to accommodate so many, particularly women and children. The areas laid out for "uninvited guests" were for the crews of freighters that would be sunk or captured. The ship had not been constructed to handle mixed passenger groups.

Furthermore, this ship was certain to send out an SOS signal if attacked, and as much as the German Admiralty might want the raider to announce her position thus, Captain Rogge had other ideas. The ship, which turned out to be the Ellerman passenger liner *City of Exeter*, was allowed to go on her way, which she did at high speed, steering north-northwest. The crew of the raider was mildly exasperated, particularly since the other ship did not offer the courtesies of the sea, a message or a dip of the ensign, or the hoisting of a signal flag. Rogge's men believed the reason was snobbishness against the Japanese they pretended to be. The actual reason was that the captain of the British ship was extremely suspicious of the "Japanese" vessel, and moved out as quickly as he could, then sent messages to British naval units suggesting his suspicions.

Next day, on the afternoon watch another ship appeared, first as a long wispy trail of smoke in the sky. As the cruiser headed on a southwest course, the other ship came up on the port side. Captain Rogge was called, he focused those heavy glasses, and then acted.

"Alarm," he shouted, and the sailors on the bridge sounded the klaxon that burst through the ship sending every man to his battle post.

"*Beide Maschinen Grosse. Kurs 110 Grad!*"—Both engines full speed ahead. Course 110 degrees.

The gunners and rangefinders were now the key men of the ship. Except for Gunnery Officer Kasch's commands and their responses, a tense silence descended on the raider. Men who could see bow-on were watching. The rest were waiting. The gunnery officer and his three enlisted men were crouched behind the canvas rail of the "water tank" that concealed the rangefinder. Only Rogge and the kimonoed Mohr stood on the bridge in sight; hidden were the quartermasters, the torpedo officer and his staff, the navigator, and a handful of signalmen.

On the boat deck below, the aircraft personnel were done up as Japanese women pushing baby carriages and strolling ostentatiously on the deck, and Lieutenant Bulla, the pilot, casually lolled on the rail in a gray flannel suit.

17,000 yards, came the call from the rangefinder.

16,000 . . .

15,000 . . .

At 14:07 the funnel of the approaching ship came up, and then the hull.

She had a red band on her funnel, she carried no flag at all, and there was a gun aft—which indicated she was an Allied merchantman armed against raiders. Her radio shack was directly abaft the funnel—a matter of grave interest to Captain Rogge and his men, for if the other ship offered resistance, or tried to run or send a message, that radio must be knocked out immediately.

At 14:37 the range had decreased to 10,400 yards—the raider was hauling up on the other ship very nicely, without appearing to take any notice of her existence.

8,000 yards . . .

7,500 . . .

7,400 . . .

7,300 . . .

Constantly, Rogge was issuing quiet orders to alter speed, so as to maintain the bearing on the other ship, which was holding steady on her old course.

Then came the moment.

Fallen Tarnung! (Drop camouflage) came the order from the captain.

The levers were pressed and the hinged flaps that concealed the guns were pulled up smartly, the crane becoming No. 3 gun and the hut on the stern falling away to show another. The signalman standing by the signal boxes ran up the flag XL (Heave to or I fire) and "Don't use your radio." The 37 mm. signal gun in the bow could not be brought to bear, so the traditional shot across the bows of the quarry was given by a 75 mm. gun.

The other ship steamed on. In a moment up came a flag, the signal for "half," which meant absolutely nothing to Captain Rogge or anyone else on the deck of the raider.

"Just like clockwork," said one seaman. (It had taken two seconds for the whole operation to be completed.)

"He'll die of shock," said someone else.

The other vessel steamed on, apparently unconcerned.

What was she doing?

Captain Rogge ordered the starboard 150 mm. guns to fire, again ahead of the other ship. The guns fired and the splashes of their projectiles sent water spouting high in the air ahead.

The merchantman steamed blithely on, hoisting her answer high, maintaining course and speed.

Raider 16 was bearing down so rapidly that Captain Rogge had to turn away to maintain the action. The other ship sent a column of steam escaping to the skies, and appeared to stop; then turned sharply to starboard and steamed away at full speed.

Immediately, Captain Rogge turned back to his old course. It was apparent that the other was going to make a run for it, and there was nothing to do but begin shooting at her.

Below in the radio shack, Radioman Helmle had the earphones pressed to his head, and he was waiting, listening.

QQQQ, came the signal. QQQQ . . . QQQQ . . .

"Unidentified merchantman has ordered me to stop."

Here was the moment for which Helmle had been trained for months. In reflex his right hand began tapping out gibberish loud and clear to drown out the QQQQ call, and at that moment he shouted for the ears of the bridge:

"Ship sending."

This sending and the turning of the quarry came all at once, in a space of 30 seconds.

Rogge lifted his glasses again.

"*Feuererlaubnis!*" (Permission to fire at will) he shouted and the order was transmitted to Gunnery Officer Kasch.

The starboard guns began to open up.

The first salvo hit aft. White and gray smoke began rising from the enemy merchantman, but still she did not stop. The second salvo hit below the bridge, to port. Flames licked up, but they could scarcely be seen from the raider, for a cloud of sulphurous yellow smoke rose up in front of the bridge, stinging the eyes of the men on the bridge.

"Halt," shouted Captain Rogge. He wanted to see what effect the fire had had, what action the enemy ship would now take. If she were a prize, to be sent home, he did not want her wrecked. Nor did he wish to cause unnecessary loss of life among men in the other ship who were, after all, merchant seamen and not military men. There was also the question of conserving ammunition, for who knew when the raider would be in a position to pick up supplies?

The smoke cleared away from the bridge of *Raider 16*.

Below in the radio shack, Radioman Helmle shouted: "*Gegner funkt!*"

The enemy was still sending that telltale QQQQ . . . QQQQ . . . QQQQ . . .

"*Feuer!*"

Now came another salvo. It missed completely!

Rogge looked inquisitively at Oberleutnant Kasch—the gunners had not missed like that in practice for months.

Another salvo went wide, and another, and a fourth.

The range-correction gear had broken down!

The Germans continued to shoot. Luckily one shell broke the radio aerial on the other ship, and the long wire went trailing down over her radio shack. Another salvo straddled the ship—one shell hit amidships. Flames rose high, and a cloud of gray and black smoke followed.

Radioman Helmle suddenly reported that the radio messages had stopped. Was it because the radio had broken down or because the Englishmen were ready to give up? Captain Rogge did not know, and not knowing he ordered the flaps lifted on the port 150 mm. guns, too. But as he turned to starboard to engage those guns, the enemy turned to port, blowing off steam in such quantity that all on the bridge knew she was blowing her boilers. A safety precaution no doubt, for her stern was in flames now, and her crew were making for the boats.

"*Halt, Batterie, halt,*" shouted the commander. There was silence, save for the lapping of the sea and the scuffling noises of the English crew as they made for the boats.

In a few moments the well-trained German crew had the motor pinnace over the side, and the boarding and detonation party began streaming into the boat. Adjutant Mohr was head of the party, and along with him came Lieutenant Fehler, the demolitions expert, and a dozen enlisted men. They were all armed with machine guns, pistols, carbines, hand grenades, signal flags and pistols, first-aid kits, and explosive charges in 30-pound boxes.

The ship was to be sunk, that much had been determined before the boarding party set off in the boat. Soon they were climbing the Jacob's ladder up to the deck of the other ship, having passed the ship's boats en route, and having been mildly surprised to discover that this English ship was manned by dark-skinned "Lascars." Only the first officer and the captain remained aboard. Adjutant Mohr met the captain on deck at the gangway and the latter gave a brief, cold, but proper salute. What ship? She was the *Scientist*, 6,200 tons, owned by Harrison and Co. of Liverpool, bound from Durban to Liverpool with a cargo of copper, chrome, and other mixed goods, including a large shipment of fiber.

Had there been any question about sinking her, it would quickly have been resolved by a look in No. 5 hold, where the ship's jute cargo was aflame, with such intensity that it could never be put out except by the sea.

Adjutant Mohr went looking for papers. All the secret papers had been jettisoned over the side, and the radio shack had been completely destroyed by the shells that struck abaft the bridge. But he did find charts and books and the contents of the chart house wastebasket, which he dumped into his seabag to take back and go over at leisure for valuable information. He also picked up binoculars, signal flags, and a chronometer. He passed one dead "Lascar" on the deck, the top of his head blown away, and he went aft, the smell of burning jute sharp in his nostrils, to examine the damage done to the ship's single gun by the 150 mm. shells. There was a gaping hole in the deck next to the gun emplacement, result of a direct hit.

Leutnant Fehler, meanwhile, was busy attending to the placement of his charges in the hull of the ship. The party also opened the seacocks, taking a long time about the unfamiliar work. Then it was time to abandon the ship to her fate.

Adjutant Mohr shepherded his men over the side, they helped the English officers into the motor pinnace, towed all the British lifeboats clear of the ship, and then lit the fuses of their charges. In ten minutes they were back aboard the raider.

The charges popped off with dull thuds but, much to Leutnant Fehler's chagrin, the ship did not sink, but simply went down a bit and developed a list. Captain Rogge ordered Oberleutnant Kasch to put some more shells into her, preferably at the waterline, and the gun crews began what was now scarcely more than target practice. But it was not until a torpedo had been sent home in the *Scientist* that she shuddered and sank. Aboard the raider, First Officer Kühn was the busiest man, supervising the housing of the officers and crew of the enemy ship. There were 20 white men aboard and 57 "Lascars." The radio operator had miraculously escaped from his wrecked radio shack with relatively minor wounds in the head and arms.

But though there were few wounded, supplies and equipment had to be issued to the enemy seamen. They must have bedding and eating utensils. They were questioned and asked to submit their documents. (This procedure was done by the book, but the Germans soon found that if the Englishmen and others knew anything, they were not telling it to the enemy, and after a few more encounters they gave up intelligence questioning as a bad job.)

Captain Rogge and his officers talked to Captain Windsor, commander of the *Scientist*, and discovered that the merchant captain had been asleep when the raider began coming up. Captain Windsor felt that fate had dealt him a low blow, because if he had been awakened and on deck, he might have turned away in time and avoided capture.

It was four hours before one could say the *Scientist* was disposed of. She was a long time in sinking, and as she went down Captain Rogge stood on his bridge and looked at her a little mournfully.

"Ships are like human beings, you know," he said to his subordinates on the bridge. "Each has a life of its own, and each dies differently . . ."

Scientist died gracefully, gently, sliding down into the deep and taking with her all the secrets she had accumulated in a ship's life. *Raider 16* steamed on proudly, looking for her next victim.

CHAPTER NINE

Minelayer

Scientist was sunk on May 3, 1940, and for the next few days Captain Rogge and his officers and men sorted out what they had learned in this baptism of fire. They steamed slowly south, along the sea-lane, making 12 knots and zigzagging a bit to take advantage of a broader bite of the lane.

They had learned a good deal. First the question of the radio had been settled: they now knew that a British ship would use her radio to try to call for help if she were attacked, and the raider must operate on the principle that this would always be the case. What was to be done? Captain Rogge decided that next time they would try shock treatment: firing several rounds simultaneously across the ship's bow and trying in that way to show the captain that it was useless to resist or to try to call for help.

Second was the discovery in the papers Mohr had picked up that most British merchant ships wore black or gray on their hulls, with upper works of brown-yellow. Captain Rogge put this information in the back of his mind. It would help him transform the raider into a British ship when necessary.

He also read with interest that British ships were to run completely blacked out at night, without even navigation lights showing. That, too, would be helpful.

In questioning the British officers, Rogge had discovered that the camouflage of *Atlantis* (*Raider 16*) was so good that the officer of the watch in the merchantman had been completely fooled as to her nationality. The captain had said he would have known her for a German but he would not say why, and so Rogge did not pay much attention to the remark.

Captain Rogge learned, too, that it would take five times as

43

much explosive as they had used on *Scientist* to sink a merchantman of 6,000 tons, and Captain Rogge issued orders that next time they were to take along 200 pounds of explosives for the job. It was wasteful to use a torpedo on a ship already captured, and he had done so only because *Scientist* took so long to go down that afternoon came upon them and he was afraid her burning hulk would bring British warships after him.

But most important of all, the men of *Raider 16* learned that *Scientist* was not due in Freetown until May 10, and that since her signals for help had been successfully jammed (the German operators had listened carefully for any response and heard none), the Germans could proceed until May 11 or 12 without suspicion of their presence. Captain Rogge had a load of mines aboard which he wished to deliver in a most conspicuous and useful place. Berlin had chosen an area around Cape Agulhas. So the raider picked up speed and headed for these waters where she would hunt big game by delayed action. *Raider 16* headed well south of the tip of Africa, turned due east to the Indian Ocean, and then doubled back toward Cape Agulhas, for she wanted her approach to the land to be that of a ship coming from Malaya or Australia. Thus, anyone who observed a Japanese passenger freighter moving from Asiatic waters to the west would not be likely to come to the conclusion that she was really a German minelayer.

For the minelaying mission, Captain Rogge would really have liked a little dirty weather but, obstinately, Mother Nature gave the Germans fine day after fine day. A light wind drove a gentle following sea, and the sun beat down cheerfully during the daylight hours while the cool winds calmed the night. There was one blessing: in World War II as in World War I, the Germans had learned to their pleasure that the Asiatics who manned British ships had no particular love for their masters or loyalty to their cause, and so it was simple enough to recruit them to work for their captors. This system relieved the Germans of guard problems and added—in this case 57 Asiatics—to the crew of the ship. Very helpful, particularly for a "Japanese" vessel. Some of the Asians chipped paint and repaired rigging, while others worked in the kitchen and the galley. One personal victory won by the captain was to get an Indian cook who knew how to prepare rice. From his younger days and visits to Far Eastern waters, Captain Rogge had developed a taste for rice dishes, but he could not abide the manner in which the usual

German navy cooks boiled up their rice into a glutinous mass. Now, for the first time in years, he had captured a good rice cook! He made the most of it, and even the Germans learned to cook rice properly under the Indian tutelage.

As the ship steamed east, and then back west, the crew prepared again for action. The fire control system was taken down and repaired, the gunners began practicing their work again in dry runs, and the whole crew was called to action stations regularly to maintain that 2-second readiness factor.

By the morning of May 10, Captain Rogge was preparing his mine run, coming from the east. He planned to be in position by 17:00 that day, to begin the run, and then to maintain a speed of 15 knots while his mine experts dropped their "eggs." He was not overly concerned about the continued good weather, because the Whitsuntide weekend was coming up, and knowing his Englishmen he was certain that even in wartime South Africa would be in a holiday mood, not inclined to be too careful about a lonely neutral ship coming into coastal waters.

In fact, the British naval defense forces in the area at the moment were far from adequate, much weaker than Captain Rogge would then have believed. The cruiser *Cornwall* was on patrol off Dakar, the cruiser *Shropshire* was in Freetown, and the cruiser *Dorsetshire* was in Simonstown—but the last was in for refit and could be written off as an effective defense weapon at the moment. Also in the general area were the light carrier *Hermes* off Dakar, the old seaplane tender *Albatross* at Freetown, and two auxiliary cruisers in transit for the South Atlantic from the United Kingdom. Nor did the inadequate number of ships suggest the British problem in its entirety. Whitehall expected war with Italy at any moment, a belief which created the report heard by Captain Rogge about diversion of convoys from Mediterranean to Cape routes, so these and other British naval vessels were very busy indeed on port protection and convoy duty. His presence still unsuspected in the area, Captain Rogge could hardly have chosen a better time for his mining venture. At 16:00 the crew went on war watch—the next state of readiness to action stations. At 17:00, as expected, the raider was in position, and as dusk rolled down the captain could see from the bridge the Cape Agulhas light 55 miles off the starboard bow. Steadily the ship moved in toward light and shore, as dusk gave way to the velvet night of the southern hemisphere, and blue water changed to shiny phosphorescence. In they moved in the setting moon, the sharp eye of the light swinging rhythmically around in front of them. They were so close to shore by 18:30 that Captain Rogge could see the headlights of a car ducking and probing through the night as the automobile sped along the mountain roads behind the light.

At 20:30 the horns sounded throughout the ship and the crew went to action stations. At 20:45 the minelaying ports on the stern lower deck were opened, and down in the mine room Leutnant Fehler glanced at his watch in the dim light and his men began horsing a black mine on the steel launching rail, its asparagus-like cluster of cables giving it a fuzzy look. The big blond Fehler picked up his telephone and reported to the bridge that all was ready, and on the bridge Captain Rogge gave his permission to begin the run. Fehler set his watch, and the work began at 21:30.

Over the black monsters went, one by one, at regular intervals. The sea gave them its benison that night: although there was only 5.5 feet of freeway between the mine ports and the waterline, only once did *Atlantis* take water through the ports. And by the time dawn began to emerge from night, the Agulhas Bank had been mined. An area reaching from within 5 miles of the Cape itself to a point 26 miles at sea had been mined in a pattern reaching from 25 to 60 fathoms—92 mines laid out in the best design that could be devised by the underwater experts in Berlin to catch the incoming and passing British ships as they rounded the Cape.

As they zigzagged, Captain Rogge gave orders to manufacture some "evidence" that the mines had been laid by a submarine. A lifebuoy was painted gray and stenciled with the identification *U-37*, and thrown overboard. Then, as the last of the mines went into the water 23 miles south of the Cape at 01:17, Captain Rogge headed for the Indian Ocean to begin his hunting once again.

Captain Rogge was an extremely careful man, and not for a moment did he fail to consider any of the factors that might inhibit the success of his mission. He had gone past his target and doubled back, to confuse any possible enemy reconnaissance and to confuse the prisoners aboard his ship. The officers of *Scientist*, even though not given the freedom of the bridge, could estimate course and speed of the raider and come to a reasonably accurate analysis of the minelaying operation—but by over-shooting and doubling back, Rogge gave them the impression that his mines had been laid hundreds of miles to the northeast, around Durban.

Rogge knew this much next day as the raider steamed toward the Indian Ocean. He also decided then that he would further confuse his captives so that when eventually they were put into a neutral port and questioned by British intelligence about what they had seen, they would give the British a completely misleading picture of *Raider 16*'s operations.

The mines were laid on Saturday night, and on Sunday morning after church services (*Gott mit uns!*) Captain Rogge gave the crew the information he deemed desirable about the minelaying, and then told them that they were to participate in a broad "act" to confuse the prisoners.

On the morning of May 12 the prisoners were all escorted off the decks of the ship where they were taking the sun, and herded into their quarters while the crewmen maintained a grave air of secrecy. A little later the ship stopped engines, Captain Rogge hailed an imaginary U-boat through his megaphone, there was a faint answer, and then the play began. The davits of the motor pinnace were dropped and the boat launched. One of the ship's diesel engines was run to maneuver the ship as though she were coming into position with another. The gangway was put out (on a level with the prisoners' quarters), an imaginary captain was piped aboard by a boatswain, and the men of *Raider 16* clambered noisily up and down ladders to give the impression of a liberty crew coming aboard from the submarine. In the wardroom there was laughter and much loud talk, several officers playing the roles of submariners, and from aft and forward there came singing that suggested the meeting of two crews far from home. A call went out for the ship's doctor, Surgeon Sprung, as if there were some emergency to treat, and the party went on for some time. Then the "captain" was piped back over the side, the noises of return were simulated, and *Raider 16*'s siren was sounded three times to say goodbye to the U-boat.

That night, circulating among the officer-prisoners, Adjutant Mohr pretended surprise at their acumen in discovering the raider's guilty secret, but he denied all without smiling. Only when he reached the bridge and conferred with Captain Rogge did he reveal that their little play had been a complete success.

CHAPTER TEN

The Good Ship Abbekerk

Captain Rogge headed *Raider 16* toward a point 41° South, 30° East, outside the shipping lanes, away from any place he might expect to encounter either quarry or hunters. The weather grew colder and the men donned sweaters and jackets as the ship headed away from the land. The captain's immediate objective was to seek solitude, so that he could overhaul the ship's peeling paint, rest up from two major military operations, and make a test flight of the ship's seaplane.

The radio crew's 24-hour watch was particularly geared these days to announcements from the British radio stations in South Africa. They heard coded messages in the recognizable British naval code, gossip and ship's traffic in the clear, and word from the various weather stations about the conditions off the South Africa coast; but not a word about their minefield.

The mines lay, swaying back and forth in the motion of the sea, until May 13, when the keeper of Agulhas Light heard an explosion seaward of his lighthouse, and looked out to see a disturbance in the sea. Perhaps a whale or a big fish had triggered off one of the mines, or perhaps some faulty device within the mine had caused it to explode. Whatever the cause, the secret was out. Next day came a second explosion, and naval headquarters at Simonstown sent an intelligence officer hastening to the area to check on these blasts.

The investigating officer was convinced, he returned to Simonstown, and at 22:00, the German operator on duty in the radio shack of *Raider 16* picked up the following:

Important. To all British and Allied merchant ships.

In view of unconfirmed reports of an explosion south of Agulhas all ships are warned to keep well clear of the Agulhas Bank . . .

Not much, but something. Captain Rogge could hope that his "eggs" had begun to do their work.

In fact they had not. On receiving the first report, Rear Admiral G. W. Hallifax had taken action at Cape Town: ordered minesweepers into the Agulhas area. On May 15 they arrived and began sweeping, without result until 17:15 when a mine exploded six miles away from the sweepers. Next morning the sweepers searched the inshore shipping route, some six miles off the Cape. Minesweeper *Aristea* exploded one mine in her sweep, and shortly afterward came upon another mine that she could not destroy.

That day South African authorities reported the existence of the minefield, and that night German naval headquarters in Berlin announced that German naval forces had laid the mines.

In the final analysis, the 92 mines laid by *Raider 16* did not sink any ships. On May 22, a minesweeping flotilla found one mine. On June 4, another flotilla swept up five more mines before being forced to quit by bad weather. Between July, 1940, and March, 1941, the British carried out nine more minesweeping operations here, but found only four more mines. One was later found beached. The other 80-odd mines were apparently sunk, destroyed by heavy seas, or detonated by the safety devices which exploded them when they broke away from their moorings. The mooring wires for these mines were very light for the turbulent water in which they were laid, and this was one reason given by British sources for the quick breakaway of the mines. Yet in spite of the failure to sink ships, the mining operation caused the British much pain and trouble. The whole area had to be swept thoroughly, and for many months ships were warned to beware of the water within 100 fathoms off Cape Agulhas.

The radio operators of *Raider 16* kept their ears to their sets, but were never to have the information they wished: confirmation of sinkings. What they did receive was the distinct impression from Berlin's behavior that they were being used as a propaganda device rather than a military command.

The success of the operation was exaggerated, and "what

particularly annoyed me," wrote Captain Rogge, "was that the enemy were derided for not being able to catch one lone raider. That may have sounded all right from an armchair in Berlin but we on board the raider saw nothing welcome in the enemy being stimulated to greater activity against us."

Contrast that behavior by Berlin with the actions of the naval high command in World War I, when the surface raiders went a-hunting. The Graf Dohna-Schlodien's *Moewe*, for example, was sent out in deepest secrecy and no word was let escape by the high command that might in the slightest compromise her. Indeed, so great were the security measures taken for *Moewe*'s success, that when she came home from her first trip, having sunk thousands of tons of British shipping, none but a handful of officers in the Admiralty even knew of her existence.

The furor fomented in Berlin could not but create new troubles for Captain Rogge and his men, and they found it hard to accept.

Their fears were justified on the night of May 20, when the radio operators intercepted a clear signal from the commander of the British naval base at Colombo, Ceylon, warning all ships of German raiders disguised as Japanese vessels. Aden, Port Sudan, and all harbors in East Africa were to be closed immediately from dusk until dawn, and ships west of 70° East were to black out completely if traveling at night.

Such warning meant that the *City of Exeter*'s captain had been heard and believed when he reported his suspicions of the innocent-appearing Japanese vessel he had encountered near the Cape of Good Hope. *Raider 16* was steaming along on a generally northeast course at about 50° East, 35° South, when the word came, and immediately Captain Rogge altered the course to due east, steamed in that direction for a time, and then moved south, to get off the Australia-Durban shipping lane he had been following. It was time to change hats.

Adjutant Mohr came to the commander's cabin with his list of alternative disguises, and Captain Rogge chose the camouflage of the Dutch motorship *Abbekerk*, the very night of the discovery that they had been unmasked.

The work of changeover began. As bad luck would have it, the transformation would have to be made in sloppy weather. So be it; it must be done.

Next morning Captain Rogge issued the orders and the crew

went to work on the massive task. They painted out the Japanese markings on the hull—and to do this work the ship had first to be canted over to port by flooding, and then when the starboard waterline was finished, to be recanted to the other side for the same treatment. The funnel that had had a red top now sported an orange band and the K was painted out. The upper bridge had to be repainted,and so did the masts, topmasts, and derricks, the ventilators and winch drums, and a dozen lesser parts of the ship: bitts, shutter frames, and smoke floats. The cipher books must be changed; the Dutch ensign and the ship's house flag had to be broken out. When finished, *Raider 16 (Atlantis)* was a minor symphony of color: brown and black, and orange, red, white, light green, and battleship gray in spots. Whatever she was, she certainly no longer looked like the *Kasii Maru*. So much had a bit of paint done, and the entire process had taken only twenty-four hours. The Germans had been very thorough; they had no photograph of the ship they wanted to pretend to be, but they did have a photostat of her, taken from a British book published in 1935, and when they were finished they had a product that very much resembled the ship *Abbekerk* described in Lloyd's register as belonging to the Vereenigde Neder-landische Scheep Vaarts My, NV. Somewhere in the world the real *Abbekerk* was sailing for the British; all Captain Rogge had to worry about was coming hull to hull with the honest article.

Once the transformation was complete, it became time to make new preparations for battle. World War II had brought a new weapon: the observation plane as the eyes of a warship. In theory, the plane would be nearly indestructible and very useful in protection of a raider. Captain Rogge set out to test the theory in practice. Leutnant Bulla, the flight officer in charge of the planes, decided that he would take his HE 114 up for a few spins, and he did so. On the first flight he was launched and stayed up for two hours, circling over a vast expanse of the Indian Ocean, without sighting a target for the ship. On the second flight he did the same. But soon it became apparent that the HE 114 was scarcely the craft for this work. Once she broke a float—and the float was as important as the plane. Once she smashed against the ship's side while being hoisted aboard after a flight, and the engine broke off from the fuselage and sank. Fortunately there was a spare engine (and a spare plane) but so imperfect was the airplane that Captain Rogge decided not to use it again except when it might be "absolutely vital" to make an aerial reconnaissance. "It would seem that the development of naval aircraft has not kept pace with other types of planes," he wrote bitterly in his log that day.

It was Captain Rogge's hope that he might be left severely alone by Berlin as raiders had been in World War I, and that thus he could wreak havoc among the unsuspecting British. But in a way, Berlin proved to be one of his most nagging enemies: on May 25, Joseph Goebbels's Ministry of Propaganda sacrificed long-term gain for short-term lying, and announced that "eight British merchantmen had been lost by the mines laid by a German raider off Agulhas." Besides this, said the ministry, three more ships were reported overdue and three minesweepers had been sunk in the cleaning up.

There was not a word of truth in the broadcast, except the devastating fact—to Rogge—that a German raider had laid the mines. He was taking every precaution to hide, and Goebbels, apparently, was going to expose him.

Captain Rogge zigged and zagged through the heavy Indian Ocean swell, searching for victims on the Durban-Batavia sea-lanes for a week without seeing anything at all. He decided that the ships must have moved off the normal sea-lanes, and that he must do the same if he was to be effective in his assignment; so he moved into shallower water, also changing over to the Australia-Mauritius sea-lane in the process.

Most officers of *Raider 16* expected it to be a short war, all the more so when the *blitzkrieg* began in May and the German army began mowing like a scythe through western Europe. Belgium fell, and then the beaches of France, and then Paris itself. Remembering the Franco-Prussian War, when the fall of Paris had meant the end of the war, and 1914, when the survival of Paris had changed the course of the war, *Raider 16*'s officers and crew were jubilant. And when the City of Lights collapsed, they broke out the champagne (officers) and beer (enlisted men) and gossiped about the coming end of the war. Only a few— Captain Rogge and Chief Surgeon Reil, and Adjutant Mohr— thought the war might be a long one. Mohr was hooted down genially when he suggested that the war would last until July, 1945. But Rogge did not hoot: he kept the beer ration down to a bottle per man because he did not know how long their supply would have to last.

One of Adjutant Mohr's special recommendations to Rogge had been the younger man's knowledge of languages, and particularly his familiarity with English. Consequently, among Mohr's many duties was that of monitoring English-language voice broadcasts for information and opinion from the English-speaking world. One night in June, listening to a San Francisco broadcast, Mohr heard that a Dutch motorship had been sunk. The commentator droned out the details and Mohr listened idly—then the commentator repeated the name—*Abbekerk*. Picking up his pad of notes, the adjutant rushed to the bridge and found Captain Rogge to deliver the bad news. What should be done? The number of disguises *Raider 16* might attempt was so limited that it was a grave disappointment to have the second now unmasked. Further, the chore of changing the ship's camouflage was nearly as wearing on the crew as an engagement with an enemy ship. Taking all this in view, and pulling from some forgotten corner the memory that the Dutch were building a whole series of *kerk*-class motorships, Captain Rogge decided to leave things as they were and proceed to find action.

Action came on June 10, when the lookout in the foretop reported a ship on the starboard beam.

Captain Rogge ordered a hard turn to starboard and they moved to intercept: Gunnery Officer Kasch estimated the range at 32,000 yards at the beginning of the chase; and as he did so the klaxons and alarm bells sounded through the ship, calling the men to action. The Asians, still busy with their paint chipping, were herded together and sent to their quarters below. Guards were posted at the entrance to the European prisoners' compartment, to be sure they did not try to come on deck.

In half an hour, Oberleutnant Kasch reported the range as 18,000 yards, and the other ship had begun to take shape.

What could she be? She carried two regular masts and seven shorter pole masts, such as a tanker might. Her funnel was well aft—a usual sign of a tanker. She carried a gun aft, but it was unmanned and trained astern, Rogge could see through his glasses. She did not seem to be paying any attention to *Raider 16*.

When Kasch reported the range at 9,000 yards, Rogge ordered the quartermasters to begin steering the ship in toward the other, trying to close the distance quickly.

But just then the other ship changed course and increased her speed, and *Raider 16*'s advantage was lost.

Rogge now debated. He could open fire from 9,000 yards, but as soon as he did so the other ship would begin radio transmissions, and from the distance, the jamming by the German ship's powerful radio might not work—listeners might be able to tell that the ships were five or six miles apart. Furthermore, Kasch's men should wipe out the radio shack with the first shot or two if the other ship would not stop, and the range was too great for that kind of shooting.

The other ship was steaming from east to west, and when Rogge's men had spotted the masts *Raider 16* was traveling in the same direction. But in the course of the chase *Raider 16* moved east of the other ship, which meant the sun was over Oberleutnant Kasch's right shoulder, an admirable condition for a gunnery officer to enjoy.

The chase had begun early in the day watch, and very soon it was apparent that it would not be a short one. The raider had 17 knots, but so, apparently, did the other ship. Only by straining and keeping the diesels running at full speed could they hope to catch their victim.

Just before 11:00 the range was 8,000 yards, still too far for good shooting. Half an hour later, after the raider kept edging around in 5-degree turns, the range was close to 5,400 yards, but then it began opening. Rogge decided to act. He turned 15 degrees to starboard.

"*Fallen Tarnung*," came the shout, and the gunflaps opened.

The torpedo men manned their four tubes.

Gunnery Officer Kasch readied the 75 mm. and the two forward 150 mm. guns for the opening salvos. The "heave-to" signal snaked up the signal mast, and the German naval ensign was broken out to replace the Dutch.

The other ship sped on, paying no attention.

Captain Rogge ordered the raider turned 25 degrees to port, thus bringing his entire starboard battery of 150 mm. guns to bear, in case he needed them.

Following the "fright" technique, a salvo was fired at the other ship. It fell short. A second salvo overshot the target—but by this time the other ship was no longer unaware of the activity behind and around her. Her gun was manned, her speed was increased if anything, and the radio men of *Raider 16* reported the ship ahead was sending a distress signal: ". . . LJUS Norwegian Motorship *Tirranna* . . ." and giving her position.

The raider's radio began flashing out a jamming signal, "VVV test VVV . . . VVV test VVV . . . VVV test VVV . . . VVV test VVV . . ." But Rogge knew *Tirranna*'s signals were getting through to the outside world, for he kept a monitoring system on his own broadcasts and the others, and monitors reported they could heart the distress call above the jamming.

So it was a Norwegian!

Just that morning Captain Rogge had learned by radio of the fall of Norway's armed forces and the capitulation of the government to the Germans, but this Norwegian did not seem to believe it. His gun fired a shot. It fell short. Then *Raider 16*'s guns began to boom.

Between salvos the Norwegian captain zigzagged, and so effective was his evasive action that the raider's gunners did not find a pattern and begin securing hits until the sixth salvo. Then the destruction began. It continued until *Raider 16* had fired 150 rounds of ammunition—30 salvos. Only then did the Norwegian ship heave to and raise a small white flag.

Adjutant Mohr led the boarding party again, along with Demolition Office Fehler. They found the main deck actually running with blood, because a party of stokers had come on deck to observe the fight, and a 150 mm. shell had plowed straight through their group. Five were dead and a score were injured.

Mohr found Captain Hauff Gunderson and walked up to him.

"But Norway made peace with you today," were that poor man's first words.

Peace with Norway, yes, under German control, but not peace for Norwegian vessels carrying cargo for Britain. Mohr, a loyal German, considered the captain's line of reasoning an odd one. But when the captain came across to the raider, Captain Rogge exhibited much more gentle behavior.

"Why didn't you stop when we hoisted our ensign and signal?"

"We never saw your flags," Captain Gunderson replied. He had been on his bridge along with his chief engineer, and as *Raider 16* came up on them, he had simply looked upon her as a Dutchman of the *kerk* class. "That Dutchman is making good speed," he had said, "but we won't let him pass us." So the Norwegian had been engaged in a friendly little race between motorships, while the German had been occupied with deadly business.

How deadly was soon discovered aboard the *Tirranna*. Most of her lifeboats were smashed. The first round had hit abaft the stern gun and the second struck the stern above the waterline. One shell exploded in the radio shack and the messroom below, another on the after section of the bridge, another forward in the crew's quarters. The ship was carrying wheat, wool, trucks, beer, tobacco, and food, and mail for the Australian Expeditionary Force in North Africa.

When Adjutant Mohr had reported his first findings, Captain Rogge had sent word that Leutnant Fehler was to stop his demolition work, because they were making a prize of the Norwegian ship. She was fast, German-built, and her cargo was valuable. Hit though she was, she had sustained relatively little damage and was entirely seaworthy.

First the wounded had to be cared for, and they were quickly transferred to the raider where the two surgeons began working over them. Captain Gunderson half expected to be shot for resisting the Germans, but Captain Rogge promised that no harm would come to him and his men. They were to be treated as prisoners of war, he said, and he was only sorry that through mischance the Norwegian ship had suffered such heavy losses in men killed and wounded.

So the prisoners were transferred—and so was some of the cargo, particularly some of the 3,000 cases of canned peaches *Tirranna* was carrying. Some 17,000 cases of jam and other foods were to be sent back to Germany, God willing.

Captain Rogge replenished his supplies with chocolate, hams, cheeses, and soap. His men searched the ship and found secret papers that had not been destroyed. They took 80 tons of fuel oil from the other motorship. Then Captain Rogge called Leutnant Waldmann to him, and gave this prizemaster instructions about the future. Waldmann would command the *Tirranna* in an attempt to take her back to Germany. He would have a crew of twelve Germans, seven Norwegians, and eight Asians, all the supplies he could use, and he would go to a rendezvous point 500 miles south of their position. He was to wait at this one position (31° 10′ South, 68° 30′ East) until August 1, unless sighted. Then he was to move to an "evasion" position, also listed. After August 1, he was to move again, and remain there until August 31. He was to play Norwegian, and complain about being chased and shot up by the Germans. If he was boarded, he was to scuttle the ship and take to the boats.

Raider 16 gave her new satellite a lifeboat to replace the damaged ones of *Tirranna*. Leutnant Waldmann repeated his orders, moved cross the open water to take charge of his new command, and in an hour the point at which they met was once more empty sea as each ship steamed about its business.

Raider 16's business at this point was to find more prizes and sink them as quickly as possible, before the defending British could send capital ships into her area of the Indian Ocean to track her down. If *Tirranna* had not been heard—and Captain Rogge had picked up no calls for her, nor any indication that other ships were coming to her rescue—then he had time. He would have to operate on that assumption.

Raider 16 now had two captures to her credit, and in them Captain Rogge had made some observations he wanted to pass along to his crew. One of Rogge's heroes was Kapitän zur See Karl von Mueller of the German cruiser *Emden*, who had begun World War I for Germany with a bang in these Indian Ocean waters by sinking more than twenty ships in a few weeks. Most notable about the *Emden*, her captain, crew, and brief life as a corsair, was that captain and crew behaved with absolute propriety in treatment of enemies. They went further than they need go—no enemy was ever manhandled, nothing was stolen from him, his wounds and illnesses were treated, and he was freed at the first opportunity, when enough such captives had collected to send them back to a neutral port in a worthless captured vessel. One could not just say that the laws of war were observed with punctilio, it must be said that von Mueller was a courageous and courteous man who preyed on ships, not people, unless he was fighting another ship of war.

Sadly enough, Captain Rogge had noted, the crewmen of *Raider 16* were not living up to the standards their captain had already set for them—the standards of the *Emden*. They sometimes laughed derisively at their enemies. More important, some members of the boarding parties had seized "souvenirs" which were in effect loot from the enemy officers and seamen. Rogge would have no more of that; on the afternoon of June

13, he called the crew together and told them so. *Raider 16* had a job to do, but she was to do it with the utmost humanity possible. From this point on, all captives were to be treated with respect and "souvenirs" would be taken only with permission of an officer.

About a week after capturing *Tirranna*, Captain Rogge grew tired of inactivity and headed for new waters. It had not been a worthless week—they had altered the look of *Raider 16* to that of *Tirranna* herself as much as possible. They darkened the hull and put on Norwegian markings which they then painted over, in the manner that *Tirranna*'s had been done, and they darkened the upper works of the ship and painted on the name *Tarifa*.

On June 16, the raider abandoned the area and set out for the point where the Australia-Aden sea-lane met that marked between Sunda Strait and Durban, and set up their patrol.

The next month was to be the test of the raider's spirit, although as the days droned by one by one, neither captain nor the crew knew how stringent the test would be. Day after day the officer of the watch wrote the same entry in the log: "Nothing sighted."

Day after day the men went about the daily routine; sleeping or reading or playing cards off watch, carrying out the usual duties of painting, scraping, washing, and repairing that are ship life, and being completely bored by it all. It was bad enough to be moving around in enemy water (for the Indian Ocean must certainly be regarded as enemy water in World War II). No one knew how long *Raider 16* must remain out. No one knew when she would be supplied, or by whom. Captain Rogge called a conference of his senior officers and asked them to draw up survival tables, to tell him how long they could stay at sea with their supplies of fuel, basic foods, and water. Yes, this was trying. More trying was the callous attitude of Berlin, which did not relay important news of the war to the ships at sea, causing Rogge to turn to other sources.

Rogge was annoyed with Berlin. Berlin was equally annoyed with Rogge, for in spite of instructions to the contrary, he would not use his radio to keep the Admiralty informed of his depredations. Other raider captains were endangering ship and crew by transmitting the information Berlin wanted. (Radio fixes brought *Raider 10* to the attention of the British at this time. She was engaged by a British auxiliary cruiser in the South

'Atlantic and suffered a narrow escape. Captain Rogge, however, simply would not risk his ship by broadcasting.)

So the days passed raggedly and tensions grew within *Raider 16*. They could hear shore stations calling up the missing *Tirranna* and they could only wonder how long it would be before searching vessels began moving into the region.

Sometimes they steamed, sometimes they shut off engines and drifted to save oil. Between June 25 and July 2, *Raider 16* lazed along in the Sunda Strait-Mauritius route, hoping to find a tanker or two.

On July 10, the raider came within 600 miles of Colombo, Ceylon, the British port and naval base, and at dawn on July 11 the ship turned westward to patrol the sea-lanes again. That morning, a month after the last engagement, the lookouts of *Raider 16* saw a smoke cloud on the horizon.

Smoke cloud? When the smoke came up midway on the morning watch it was so thick that at first the lookout believed they had sighted a convoy. If so it would be hands off, for Berlin's sailing orders had stipulated that the raiders would give a wide berth to convoys. But Captain Rogge was a careful man and he did not jump to conclusions. The alarms sounded, the crew leaped to action stations, and the captain ordered the engines stopped so he could peer carefully through his binoculars. (One of the complaints about *Raider 16* was that her engine vibration was so great that the captain found it difficult to use his binoculars effectively when she was moving.)

The morning haze lay sprawled like moss across the sea, and through it appeared a pair of masts, and then another pair on the other side of the smoke. It was one ship, moving slowly toward them and paying no attention. Captain Rogge ordered the first diesel started, and then the second, for he wanted full speed as soon as it could be achieved. As the ship worked up its rpms Rogge began edging toward the other vessel, and their convergence soon brought her into sight. She was a single-funneled ship of dark hull and brown upper works like so many British freighters. Although she flew no flags, she *was* British, the telltale marks were all there, especially in the peculiar after gun platform that the British installed on their freighters. But she was something else as well, as one of the officers noted. She was a German-built ship, once of the Hansa Line, this officer suggested.

On the morning watch there was a regular period for the receipt of distress signals, and all ship and shore installations in the area listened in on the assigned frequency during that time. *Raider 16* was moving in on the big freighter (she was 7,500 tons) just at this time and it would be very dangerous to strike just then. So Captain Rogge sweated and waited through the radio silence. When the welcome sound of high-speed transmissions and hand transmitters began again, the radio room signaled the bridge, and Captain Rogge prepared to swing into action. Long since he had abandoned the 37 mm. signal gun in the bow as an ineffective device to stop a vessel. This day he ordered four warning shots fired from the 75 mm. gun, as the German flag and the stop signal were run up.

The other ship acknowledged the stop signal—but began sending with her radio:

"QQQQ shelled by ra- . . ."

They were at 3,000 yards, and the moment that the radio began to sound the raider's operators informed the captain. The next salvo sent across made a direct hit on the radio room, and another shell shattered the mast and destroyed the aerial. *Raider 16*'s radio men began jamming the airwaves, using Japanese call signs. But it was too late. Somewhere in the world the American steamer *Eastern Guide* had picked up the distress signals and the fragmentary message, and its operator was not to be fooled.

"Who shelled by?" came the query from *Eastern Guide*.

The raider's quarry did not answer—she could not. *Raider 16* sent a brusque message: "ORU"—I have nothing for you.

"Stop transmitting," said *Eastern Guide*, when *Raider 16* had repeated the QRU signal a number of times. "Who shelled by?"

Fortunately for Captain Rogge's peace of mind, just then a British shore station broke into the conversation, repeating the QRU signal several times, and *Eastern Guide* gave up the talk.

Meanwhile, the crew of the ship under attack began frantically moving to get into the boats and abandon ship. The Germans had signaled them to remain on their vessel, but too many of these seamen knew the stories of friends who had been sunk by the Germans and left to sink or swim. (These sinkings were almost entirely the work of submarines to this date, but the sailors were in no position or mood to differentiate between a gallant Captain Rogge and a murderous U-boat captain.) As usual the dapper Adjutant Mohr was chief boarding officer. He and his men swarmed up the gangway, he carrying a heavy Mauser pistol as always, and trailed by Leutnant Fehler, demolition expert, and the signalmen who would report what they had found and await Captain Rogge's decision as to whether the ship should be destroyed or taken as a prize.

Adjutant Mohr walked briskly to the captain's cabin. He found Captain Armstrong White stooped over his desk ransacking the drawers to be sure he had destroyed his papers.

The room was a wreck, for the shell which had struck the radio shack had also torn down the partition between that enclosure and the captain's office. The captain stood, back to Mohr, and grubbed in the papers.

"A little untidy, sir?" said Mohr.

"Yes, I suppose it is," said the captain, not turning.

"An awful mess, Captain."

"And a fool thing to say," snapped the captain—then turning, he saw the German uniform and fell silent.

The white-haired captain seemed to have done a better job than most merchantmen in destroying the secret papers of his trade, but some were found, because in the rush of the attack he had had to supervise the men personally in their panic, and could not do two things at once.

Mohr pointed the pistol and told the captain he was a prisoner, and the captain went on deck. There he found his crew, for the Germans had forced them to come back aboard the ship and get the belongings they had abandoned in their fear.

Mohr quickly learned that he had boarded the *City of Baghdad*, once the Hansa liner *Geierfels*, but at this time the property of the British Ellerman Line. He discussed the question of sinking or salvation with Captain Rogge, and it was decided— the ship was old, dating from 1919—that she must be sunk.

As was usual with raiders in both wars, *Raider 16* was to live on her captures, and from *City of Baghdad* she took potatoes for the Germans and rice for the Asians before setting about the task of sinking the ship. Mohr finished his work and went back to the bridge of *Raider 16* to report to Captain Rogge and begin going through what papers he had found on the enemy ship. Leutnant Fehler remained aboard the *City of Baghdad* to set his demolition charges.

Fehler was ashamed of the failure he had suffered in the case of *Scientist*, and he was determined to have nothing go wrong with the sinking of this new ship. Captain Rogge had suggested that he increase the total number of charges to add up to 200 pounds of explosive, distributed through the bottom of the ship. In order to avoid any mistakes at all, Fehler decided to increase the charge to 260 pounds and to stay on the spot and watch results himself. Usually, of course, the demolition party set short fuses but allowed themselves plenty of time to be over the side and away from the victim ship before the charges blew. This time Fehler remained on deck.

From the bridge of the raider, Captain Rogge and Adjutant Mohr watched as the demolition party pulled away from the enemy, and then stopped. The captain was puzzled until he searched the boat with his glasses.

"Where the devil is Fehler?" he asked.

Mohr looked, but he could not see the lieutenant either. Then, a moment later, came the bump-bump of the explosive charges going off. As the ship took a heavy list and began to sink by the stern, Fehler appeared on deck, the boat came back for him, and he hastened over the side—so rapidly he suffered a nasty cut on the arm in getting down.

Captain Rogge was not pleased. Fehler was assigned as demolition expert, not daredevil, and the captain went to some pains to explain that fact to his junior officer.

As the captain "chewed out" the younger officer, the ship was heading at high speed toward the south, to escape the dragnet Rogge fully expected to be flung by the British. He was certain that the American master of *Eastern Guide* had not been fooled, even though he had been unable to confirm his suspicions in the matter of the *City of Baghdad*. That ship had been sunk almost on the equator at 86° East, which meant the raider was about halfway between Ceylon and Sumatra, in the waters where *Emden* had worked so successfully in World War I.

Other raiders were now coming out to sea. *Orion* had gone into the Pacific after rounding the Horn. *Widder* had gone into the North Atlantic. *Thor* had set out for the South Atlantic, and *Pinguin* had also come to the Indian Ocean. Perhaps most interesting of all the outward-bound voyages was that of *Komet*, which went through the Northeast Passage, escorted by two Russian ice-breakers, passed through the Bering Strait, and entered the Pacific Ocean. The more raiders the better, it would seem.

CHAPTER ELEVEN

Tirranna *Goes Home*

Heading south, away from the scene of her latest action, the crew of *Raider 16* (*Atlantis*) relaxed a little in those early July days, but not the captain. He was busy, as always, sharpening up the performance of his ship and crew on the basis of mistakes made on the last operation. He made several changes in procedure: most important was the advice to Lieutenant Kasch to use his 150 mm. guns from now on to fire warning shots, and waste no further time on the 75 mm. The problem that bedeviled Rogge was that which upset all raiders and U-boat captains: if they gave sufficient warning to the enemy without instilling the idea that capture was imminent and absolutely certain, the attacked ships were sure to use their radios. Steeped in the tradition of naval gallantry of the past. Captain Rogge found it difficult to consider firing first and talking afterward. Also, it was not an unimportant matter to capture cargo ships for his own use and others to be sent back to Germany. So he was working constantly to refine his techniques and speed up the process of forcing a surrender.

Among the papers found by Mohr on the *City of Baghdad* was a description of a suspect ship, sighted by the *City of Exeter*. Rogge read this with interest, for the ship in question was no less than his own, and the description, accompanied by pictures of a similar Hansa liner, was remarkably apt. The answer was to make more changes in the look of *Raider 16*. Captain Rogge ordered his carpenters to build extra gallows masts fore and aft from empty barrels. It made a nice, definable change in the profile of the ship.

So they moved on, southwest, until on the morning of July

13 they were 3 degrees below the equator, at about 81° East, when the forward lookout sighted a smoke cloud to port, and the sighting was confirmed that very moment by the lookout in the mainmast. To avert suspicion, Captain Rogge turned 20 degrees to port and began to move, nervously, asking the radio shack constantly if the enemy was beginning to transmit. Each time the answer was the same: the enemy was quiet, although there were noises suggesting that someone on the other ship was tuning a transmitter in preparation for sending.

Captain Rogge ordered Gunnery Officer Kasch to open fire on signal with every gun possible, and to aim to destroy the other ship's radio. Slowly, at 9 knots, the raider moved in on the unsuspecting merchantman.

At 10:09 the action began, when *Raider 16* was 5,400 yards from the other ship. The order to drop the camouflage rang out, and immediately afterward came the command to commence firing.

The first four salvos missed, then the gunners found the mark with the fifth salvo and the sixth. The other ship hoisted the K flag—meaning "I am stopping," and Captain Rogge congratulated himself on his new tactic: the enemy was surrendering without making any attempt to use her radio.

The raider closed in on the other ship. On his bridge Captain Rogge stood, binoculars in hand, and watched the manning and launching of the lifeboats. The other ship was afire on the bridge deck, and a broken steampipe somewhere below was letting forth gouts of vapor which drifted above to dissipate in the air. She turned, and Rogge could read her name, *Kemmendine*.

Without warning, from the nearing stern of the *Kemmendine* came a report and a shell whizzed across the bridge of the raider.

Rogge was furious.

"*Salvos!*" he shouted.

Gunnery Officer Kasch ordered his men to begin firing again, and they blanketed the stern of the offending vessel.

On the bridge, Navigator Kamenz spoke up.

"There's only one man on the gun," he said, It might be some kind of mistake.

Captain Rogge was still angry, but he listened.

"Cease fire," he ordered. And in a few moments Adjutant Mohr was on his way to the side of the enemy ship.

She was a combination freighter-passenger vessel, and from the loaded boats it could be seen that she was carrying women and children. Rogge became even more irritated when he saw this, for the idiot gunner had very nearly put him in the position of firing on women and children.

Aboard the *Kemmendine*, Adjutant Mohr was investigating conditions and looking for papers. He found the dining room ablaze, and when he headed for the purser's cabin, he was cut off by a wall of smoke and flame. Leutnant Fehler was there, but the ship was burning so briskly that the Germans barely had time to dump the explosive charges over the side and make their escape from the decks.

Mohr returned to the bridge of *Raider 16* and reported that the ship could not be saved, nor could they go below to set charges. So she would have to be destroyed by gunfire or torpedoes. Captain Rogge chose torpedoes.

The first shot hit high, and so did the second, but their combined force broke the back of *Kemmendine* and in a few minutes the two halves sank, even as the survivors brought their boats alongside the raider and boarded.

Among the survivors were the captain, 26 white officers and men, 86 Asians, 5 white women passengers, 2 children, and 28 Indian passengers. She was an India-Burma Line boat, bound for Rangoon, and perhaps the reason she burned so fast was that she was carrying a cargo of whiskey.

The boats were destroyed, sunk, and as *Raider 16* steamed away southwest that afternoon, Captain Rogge held a court of inquiry to discover just who had fired that shot after *Kemmendine* had surrendered, and why. The court included Rogge, Navigator Kamenz, Adjutant Mohr, and Captain R. B. Reid of the *Kemmendine*. The man who had fired the shot was by trade a London window cleaner, in the service for the duration of the war. He had been aft when Captain Reid had ordered the gun abandoned, and the noise of escaping steam from that broken pipe had drowned out the captain's order. Meanwhile, not seeing the man at the gun, Captain Reid had stopped engines, run up the "heaving-to" flag, and given orders to abandon ship. It was a matter of thorough confusion in a war situation, and there was no irresponsibility about it as Rogge had at first believed.

Captain Rogge cruised south of the Chagos Islands, planning to turn south toward the rendezvous spot where he was to meet

Tirranna. Here in the Indian Ocean, *Raider 16* had done what was expected of her: she had sunk three ships and captured one, for a total of about 30,000 tons of shipping, and she had spread terror through the region, particularly in the capture of *Kemmendine*, for this ship was well known in the Asiatic trade, and many of those aboard were either wives or relatives of high officials of the Burmese government. Now, the raider would look for more.

On the day after the sinking of *Kemmendine*, Captain Rogge sent his first message back to Berlin. He had been out for three and a half months, and in spite of orders to report regularly he had refused to break radio silence in fear that the British might use radio direction to spot his position. But here in the Indian Ocean he felt he had to comply. He sent a message giving position (6° South, 77° East), noting that he had supplies for 85 more days and the tonnage he had sunk. At about this time, Rogge also announced something he had learned from the radio, that *Raider 16* had been allocated thirty second-class Iron Crosses for her work up to July 10. This allocation of medals to a ship by the high command was an old German practice, dating back to before World War I. The captain was to pass out the medals, but in this case there were no medals to pass out because when authorities at Wilhelmshaven had suggested that Rogge take a supply of Iron Crosses along with him, the captain had grimaced and said it would be best to wait until the ship had done something to earn an Iron Cross or two. So, in announcing the awards to the crew, Rogge simply said the crosses belonged to everyone and would be given out at the end of the voyage.

Two of those crosses most certainly would go to the radio officers Oberleutnant Wenzel and Funkmaat Wesemann, for this pair had succeeded in making hunting much easier for Captain Rogge. When the *City of Baghdad* was captured and Adjutant Mohr walked out of the captain's cabin with the contents of the wastebaskets and desk drawers in the seabag he carried for this purpose, Mohr had taken off a copy of the Merchant Navy Code. Using this code, Wenzel and Wesemann tried to decipher the current signals circulating in the airs of the Indian Ocean. Wesemann was well equipped for the task, having spent three years as a cryptologist. Two long signals were picked up and used as tests, and soon Captain Rogge was reading much of the confidential traffic between ship and shore stations.

At the moment, this information was valuable but not immediately useful, because *Raider 16* was preparing to rendezvous with *Tirranna*. With some 300 prisoners aboard, eating heartily, Captain Rogge's stewards and cooks were beginning to feel the pinch, and besides it made the captain uneasy to have a ship filled with prisoners as he went about his raiding business.

As for the prisoners, they were kept comparatively happy by the crew, from the children, who occupied an improvised kindergarten of sand at the base of the dummy hatch, to the lady passenger who kept a bottle of Scotch whiskey in her cabin, to the captains of the merchant vessels, some of whom had cases of whiskey transshipped from their vessels before they were sunk.

Captain Rogge had a little Scottish terrier aboard, Ferry, the ship's mascot, who came to play with the children every day.

There were some problems with the housing for the prisoners, as the crowd grew. The Germans were meticulous in observing the "white man's" way of life. Officers were in their own quarters. The European sailors were together. The Chinese kept to themselves as did the Indians, and one strict Indian kept his whole family in purdah all the time they were aboard the vessel. When the European ladies and children complicated matters by appearing on the *Kemmendine*, they were given a cabin of their own in the forecastle, in quarters equipped with six bunks, two tables, a pair of benches, and a washbasin. And the ladies had another problem: the end of the *Kemmendine* had come so quickly they had had no time to go below and salvage any clothing. So they borrowed clothing from the officers and from the ship's stores, and some were converting cotton athletic shirts to ladies' underwear.

Among the lady prisoners was one, a Mrs. Hilton, the Germans simply did not understand, because she was much more friendly to them than most. She kept telling Rogge privately that she was Irish, not English, but the nuance was lost on the captain.

There were many parties in the wardroom these days, as the Germans found more and more to celebrate, and the ladies were always invited, along with the merchant officers. But the merriment came to an end on July 29 when the raider found *Tirranna* at the rendezvous point.

Several things were to be done here. *Tirranna* was to be given 400 tons of diesel fuel for the long trip home. The prisoners were to be loaded off on the merchantman. *Raider 16* was to stop here and make some minor repairs, while Chief Engineer Kielhorn supervised an overhaul of the two big engines.

Boats were put over the sides of both ships, and the transfer of supplies and people began. Thus the next few days were as busy as any spent by the crew of *Raider 16* since they had left Germany.

But on the fifth day the gaiety that accompanied the movement of supplies and prisoners came to a sudden end. The transfer of supplies was nearly completed when Adjutant Mohr went aboard the *Tirranna* for a routine visit. There he discovered that the eleven-man German prize crew had broken into the mailbags aboard the ship, rifled them for valuables, and had thrown the mail overboard. Rogge took a dim view. Court-martial was ordered.

This straitlaced captain took an even dimmer view of the reported theft of a pair of binoculars from the captain of the *City of Baghdad*. When Rogge learned of this theft, he invited the guilty party to return the glasses without punishment, but they were not returned. Then he began talking of sterner measures against the whole crew, and someone put a note in a locker to the effect that the binoculars had been thrown overboard to avoid detection. Soon the guilty man was found by comparing the handwriting of the note with that of the crew members, and once found Captain Rogge had no mercy for the culprit. He was called before a court-martial consisting of Mohr, Pilot Bulla, and the ship's boatswain. He confessed and was found guilty, then was sentenced. He would be given two years' imprisonment in Germany, a dishonorable discharge from the navy, and he must pay Captain Armstrong White for the binoculars. He was to be shipped home on the next prize to start his sentence.

Such strict discipline had a bracing effect on the crew, who were becoming lax in their treatment of the prisoners and their belongings. Again Captain Rogge laid down the rules about "souvenirs," and this time he made arrangements for the ship's officers to collect souvenirs from the ships *Raider 16* captured, and give them out in an orderly fashion.

The transfer of oil did not proceed as smoothly as could be hoped. Captain Rogge grew a little nervous when the raider had been sitting for several days in one spot in the sea, and decided to accomplish the fuel transfer as the two ships moved toward Madagascar and Mauritius. Two 9-inch hawsers were run between the ships and the fuel lines attached, with *Raider 16* in front and *Tirranna* trailing along behind her. But almost as this was done, the wind freshened, rising from Force 4 to Force 7 in an hour and pushing a heavy swell. The working of wind and swell soon began to strain the hawsers and the ships parted before 10 per cent of the fuel had been transferred.

With a big storm brewing, there was nothing further to be done that day, and all night long the two ships lay hove to in the heavy seas, pelted by rain and whipped by winds that tore hungrily at the rigging.

Navigator Kamenz drew on his many years of experience as a merchant captain and devised a plan which Captain Rogge accepted. Next morning, when the storm had quieted and the swell had decreased commensurately, the two ships began steaming along side by side. A boat carried a small line across from *Raider 16* to the *Tirranna*. A 7-inch hawser was tied on, and carried back, and then a 6-inch steel towing wire was tied from the raider to the hawser and again hauled back. The ships were secure again, the fuel line was transferred, and a total of 450 tons of diesel oil was transferred from the raider to her captive—all the rest of this in three and a half hours.

First Officer Kühn was known privately to the crew as Captain Bligh after nearly five months at sea, and during this period he showed why. Scaffoldings were put up on *Raider 16* and painters perched in the rigging and on the masts and hung over the sides, burning off the old paint and putting on new, tightening, riveting, replacing.

On August 2 the work was proceeding along toward the noon hour, when suddenly someone aboard *Tirranna* sighted a masthead approaching at high speed and sounded the ship's siren to attract the attention of the raider. In a moment the work parties were scrambling to action stations. One engine was still down, but the other was started, and the ship began moving, the stages along her sides canting crazily in the wind, and a solitary sailor in a dinghy rowing to try to catch up.

The other ship came on steadily and swiftly, and soon Captain

Rogge saw she was manning a gun at her stern. He opened his mouth to shout for Lieutenant Kasch, and then remembered that the gunnery officer had gone aboard the *Tirranna* to supervise repairs.

So when the shooting began, it was ragged. The first salvo missed by 400 yards, but the second was a straddle, and the third scored at least one hit—which could be seen as a solid red flash.

The enemy crew abandoned their gun, and Rogge stopped the firing. Then the enemy manned the gun again and he resumed. But in a few minutes it was all over, and *Raider 16* moved in on the other. At that moment—precisely—the other ship moved into a rain squall, and it was ten anxious minutes for Rogge and his men before they came out and found her, lying to and offering no further resistance.

This ship, as it turned out, was the *Talleyrand*, 6,732 tons, bound from Sydney to England. She was the sister ship of *Tirranna!* And that coincidence also was much of the cause of her being captured at all. Her second mate was on watch that morning when he had seen a silhouette that looked like *Tirranna* alongside another ship, and from the activity going on he gathered that the two merchant ships were working on some project—perhaps one had engine trouble. So he had brought *Talleyrand* up to give a hand.

There was a pleasant if not overjoyous reunion of Captain Foyn of the *Talleyrand* and his old friend Captain Gunderson of the *Tirranna* in the prisoners' quarters of *Raider 16*, and the raider picked up another 36 prisoners of war. As for cargo, the *Talleyrand* was carrying wool, wheat, steel bars, and teak—some of it valuable enough to the German war effort. And yet Captain Rogge must make the inevitable decision: sink or send home, not on the basis of the value of the cargo, but considering whether or not the ship would have a reasonable chance of reaching German territory successfully. In this case, the captain's decision had to be No—for *Telleyrand* carried only 400 tons of fuel in her tanks. She had been scheduled to stop off in Cape Town for refueling and refitting before proceeding on to England. So it was decided that all valuables should be taken from her—adding two months' supplies to *Raider 16*—and that she would be sunk. The crew was transferred to *Tirranna*. The raider took one motorboat and 420 tons of diesel fuel into her own tanks. Captain Foyn took several bottles of whiskey into *Tirranna* so that he and Captain Gunderson would not go dry on the voyage home, and preparations were made to sink *Talleyrand*. She was scuttled by Leutnant Fehler and his men. They had grown so adept at their job by this time that the scuttling charges took only eight minutes to send the *Talleyrand* to the bottom.

Soon Lieutenant Waldmann, prize officer of the *Tirranna*, was on his way, warned to stay away from other ships, and be extremely careful in passing Cape Finisterre. He was to make for St. Nazaire, or Lorient at a pinch; Rogge had worked out a course that would keep him outside German submarine patrol areas, and, hopefully, also outside those of the English.

And so, just after midnight on August 5 the sirens of the *Raider 16* raised and howled in farewell and off went *Tirranna* to the homeland, carrying 18 men from *Raider 16* and 273 prisoners. Even as the ships parted, a strange quiet descended on the raider, for she had lost most of her unwilling passengers, and had to get back to work.

CHAPTER TWELVE

The Business of Killing

Once *Tirranna* was out of the way, taking the bulk of the prisoners of war, *Raider 16* settled down to finish her homemade refit, while Captain Rogge planned for the future. His plans were helped along considerably on August 8 when Radio Officer Wenzel reported a signal sent in the clear from Mauritius. In the future, said the British Admiralty, any ship which heard a distress signal being jammed was to signal *its own* position at once, and then try to give a bearing on the distress call and the jamming.

So—the British were getting ready to tell Captain Rogge just where their merchant ships lay. He could not have asked for more.

Those orders show the desperate straits to which British naval strategy was reduced in this period. Earlier, when the German pocket battleship *Graf Spee* and others had gone out, the British had organized hunting groups of warships. But in the summer of 1940, Britain's forces had to be spread so thin that all the Admiralty could do was escort the important convoys carrying troops from the Dominions and India to the Middle East and Europe, and to patrol other areas of shipping with armed merchant cruisers and other ships as they were available. It was reported that the British had some thirty auxiliary cruisers in the Indian Ocean at this time, but if that were true, none of them was close enough to identify *Raider 16*. Her presence in the Indian Ocean was sometimes suspected, but not proved.

Joyfully, then, Captain Rogge accepted this new challenge with refurbished engines that made 17 knots without a tremor. On August 11 he set out again on the hunt, following the

Australia sea-lane east along the route taken by *Tirranna* and the *City of Baghdad*. He heard only the signals of far-off ships and he saw nothing at all.

Nearly two weeks passed. Captain Rogge and his officers grew nervous and restive in the absence of action. They also grew very wary, for they knew it was time the British began to suspect their presence, and having great respect for their British enemies, the Germans expected opposition of some kind.

Thus when, at 03:00 on August 24, the lookout on the starboard wing of the bridge saw a vessel moving very, very slowly, he was suspicious.

She was on the starboard side, coming in, slow and black.

"Silhouette, bearing green one zero," he shouted.

And the bridge awoke to action.

Captain Rogge came to his command bridge and raised his night glasses. The other ship was dark and could barely be seen. But there she was. What was she—that was the question. One lookout said she was a destroyer. Another said she was an aircraft carrier. The chief coxswain said she was an ordinary merchant ship—but that was questionable because she had a long flat deck.

Rogge gave orders to track her and raced along at 14 knots on her trail. *Raider 16* lost her quarry in a squall, then came out and found it again. Suddenly Rogge noticed that the other ship had dropped from perhaps 5 knots to just about a knot.

He peered through his glasses. Very suspicious.

He was convinced that she was a merchant ship, but that did not mean she might not be a Q-ship, one of those heavily armed bait ships used by the British with considerable success in World War I. The Q-ship's job was to appear to be a limping or tired merchantman, then to lure into close range a raider or submarine, and suddenly to drop her camouflage and show herself to be a fully equipped, heavily armed man-of-war. As the Germans were masters of the surface raider in these wars, so the English were masters of the Q-ship technique, and a nervous Rogge was very much concerned.

For two hours Rogge shadowed the other ship, observing her strange behavior. An ordinary merchant ship in wartime would never act thus. She must be an armed merchant cruiser. Her behavior so fascinated Rogge that he continued to track until after five A.M. Suddenly he realized that dawn was sneaking up on him, that the sun would come up at 06:45 and that he had no time to disappear over the horizon in case he wanted to evade this mystery ship.

So, in a way, his decision was made for him. He must attack. He had convinced himself that this was an auxiliary cruiser—and dangerous.

Raider 16 began to maneuver for position. Captain Rogge hoped that by 05:30, when the first lights of dawn began to come through, the enemy would be outlined against the eastern sky, but at that time the ship turned to port and assumed a course parallel to *Raider 16*'s own.

Rogge considered. He was certain that this ship was too suspicious to attack in the usual way. He would launch a head-on attack.

At 05:30 he increased the raider's speed to 8 knots and in a few minutes was only 3,000 yards from the enemy. At this point he ordered a torpedo fired. It missed. The captain shouted at Gunnery Officer Kasch to open fire with his 150 mm. guns. The first salvo scored three hits out of four, the ship's bridge shot up in flames and so did the section midships. The crew ran for the boats, not even manning the gun on the poop.

Captain Rogge had been wrong, it was obvious. This ship was an ordinary merchantman—or had been. Now she was burning like a dry barn, and the men were throwing themselves off her, not even getting the boats off. Rogge moved to within 300 yards and saw what he had done. He stopped his boarding party—the fire on the deck of the other was too severe, too far gone for boarding. Adjutant Mohr was diverted, along with the other motorboats, to pick up suvivors.

The flames were leaping up above, and the waves were 10 and 12 feet high at the side of the stricken ship, so the process of rescue was not an easy one. As the boats from *Raider 16* moved in, the bridge structure of the other ship collapsed with a smashing sound and a shower of spark and flame.

Floats and wreckage were being thrown over the side and men were going to them. But the process was slow—it seemed endless to Captain Rogge, who realized they were in the middle of a major shipping lane and that they had lighted up the water with a blaze that could be seen for at least 50 miles.

The rescue work continued in the light of the burning ship, and as the survivors came aboard the story began to come out.

The ship was the *King City*, a freighter of 4,744 tons, carrying coal for the British Admiralty from Wales to Singapore. As to her actions, why they were nothing more or less than the troubles of a stricken vessel. She was rated at 9 knots, but for days she had been making scarcely half that, and this morning one of her ventilators had failed and she had come to a stop altogether—thus all the slowing and stopping that had frightened the men of the raider. It had been repaired, and then broke down again. *King City*, said the survivors, had only seen *Raider 16* three minutes before the beginning of the surprise attack. The three shells had hit the bridge and the crew's quarters, wounding the second mate in his bunk, killing four cadets who were trapped in a blazing cabin beneath the bridge, and killing a cabin boy. The survivors were the master and 26 Europeans, and 12 "Lascars" from Goa and Aden. Two of the Englishmen were wounded, and one died later on the operating table of the German ship.

Soon the rescue work was finished, and since that was all that could be done, the *King City* was sunk by shelling from a range of 300 yards and less, the shells hitting so hard that splinters bounced back on the raider herself. The gunfire tore huge holes in the sides of the ship, coal poured out into the sea, and in ten minutes the ship capsized and lay on the sea botton up like a great fat whale before she went down with her dead.

The men of *Raider 16* returned from this struggle with bad tastes in their mouths. They had witnessed a new face of war, and it was not a pleasant one. Captain Rogge was also subdued, for what had happened was scarcely in the tradition of Captain von Mueller of the *Emden*. Here was Rogge, a humane and decent man, put in the position of killing the innocent because of his own fears for the safety of his vessel. To be sure it was war, and the innocent were enemy innocent—but in the case of the *King City* they had done nothing at all to provoke attack.

War, the men of *Raider 16* learned that day, was a very dirty business. It was a measure of the humanity of this captain and this crew that the officers noticed and were ashamed when attacked verbally by their prisoners.

"You were too trigger-happy in *King City*'s case," said one prisoner to Adjutant Mohr. "She never had a chance. You shot a sitting duck, and your very first shell killed four apprentices asleep in their bunks. Another is dead now and there's a man in the sick bay who's got his stomach ripped out. He's married. He was aching to get home to the little son he's never seen. Nice, don't you think?''

Mohr's first reaction was anger. But his second was a kind of sickness. And that day, as the German officers met in the silence of their wardroom, they agreed that they wished they had never seen the *King City*.

But modern war had no place for such sentiment, as the men of *Raider 16* were to learn again very soon.

Three days after the *King City* affair, Captain Rogge learned that he was not the only German commander in the Indian Ocean. On August 27, while waiting eagerly to hear from *Tirranna*, his radio men intercepted a British distress call from the tanker *British Commander*, and he guessed that the raider *Pinguin*, which was scheduled for the Indian Ocean, had at last arrived. This coming meant new danger and new opportunity— danger because the British would soon enough guess that there was more than one raider in the area, and opportunity because *Pinguin* and *Raider 16* could now work together, sending false signals and positions to confuse the British defenders of the Indian Ocean.

Signals—communication—was coming to play an ever larger role in *Raider 16*'s life, as Captain Rogge had known it would do in this modern war.

Rogge's communications problem of the moment was to inform Berlin, unmistakably, that *Tirranna* was coming into European waters, so the Admiralty would be looking for her and protect her from harm. One message sent by *Raider 16* was received in Berlin, but the operator was careless and missed the date of arrival by a month. It took another, longer message to get the word through.

Then, on September 9, *Raider 16* was searching on the Mauritius route when her lookout sighted a yellow funnel some 14 miles away, and soon the ship came into view as a tanker with the telltale rear-slung funnel.

The problem was to keep from sending many of these long messages, lest the British in the Indian Ocean triangulate the points of suspicious QQQQ calls and undecipherable code messages and thus figure out the general area and course of the raider. So far this had not happened. Rogge was guarding against the possibility, but of course to guard completely he would have to stop attacking ships with radio stations, and that was his mission in life. The trouble was, he found that there was scarcely enough shipping to satisfy him.

The other ship was not at all suspicious. A rain squall drifted across the otherwise calm sea and interposed itself between the ships—which gave the raider a chance to move to within 8,500 yards of the tanker without appearing to be chasing. But when *Raider 16* came out of the squall, and the other ship saw her that close, she manned her rear gun, and turned onto a course parallel to that of the raider—to be sure that the ship came no closer. Captain Rogge played coolly, holding his course and pretending to see nothing. For seven minutes the other ship steered alongside him, the captain knowing that he was moving off his own course every minute, and then suspicion was allayed and the other ship dropped back, according to the rules of the road, to pass behind the raider and regain her original course.

There was good reason for Captain Rogge's calmness. He did not want to attack during the International Distress Call period, which had not yet expired as he came up on the tanker. So *Raider 16* loafed along, hoping to attract no more attention for the moment. And she did not. The other captain ordered his men from the guns, and steamed along on his own business. He hoisted the British ensign for a time, but the raider ignored the gentle request for an ensign of her own (she was flying none). The three minutes at the end of the hour for distress signals soon expired, and immediately *Raider 16* opened fire at 6,800 yards, using her shock technique to prevent the other from sending a message. The first salvo was short. The second salvo straddled the other ship.

And then the other began sending her QQQQ. . . .QQQQ. . . .QQQQ . . .

Raider 16 began jamming, and the gunners worked even faster.

Just then the raider's electric rudder circuit broke down, the helm jammed to starboard, and the attacker began circling to the right. The technicians fussed with the wiring for a bit, and then Rogge sent men aft to steer mechanically on the emergency system, and the ship answered the helm. All this time the gunners were firing, albeit erratically. When the other ship saw the raider back under control, her captain manned his gun and began returning fire. The tanker fired three times without hitting the raider, but all this while the British ship's radio was banging out the QQQQ. . . .QQQQ. . . .QQQQ. . . .and her position

This had to be stopped.

The raider's guns roared again and again, until one direct hit silenced the gun. Then the radio stopped transmitting, too, and up went the flat W which signified that she needed medical assistance.

"DR," signaled Rogge—I am coming to your assist.

Raider 16 moved close to the other ship, and Adjutant Mohr and his boarding party made ready to go over the side in their motorboat.

Then Radio Officer Wenzel reported. "The enemy is transmitting again," he shouted.

"Open fire," yelled Captain Rogge.

The guns began to blast.

At that short range there were no misses. Each shot sent up a gout of smoke and flame and debris. In a minute the bridge and stern of the other ship were ablaze. That was lamentable, because Rogge had hoped dearly to be able to siphon off enough fuel oil to fill his tanks. But war was war.

The radio transmission continued and so did the guns. Suddenly from Wenzel came another call.

"Mistake! Mistake! It's another ship."

The boarding party went over the side, and a few minutes later the signalman accompanying Mohr sent the following:

"Engine room burning. Oil in bilges has caught fire. Flames reached bridge. Oil leaking from safety valves. Risk of major explosion."

So there was the end of Captain Rogge's dream of refueling. The ship, *Athelking*, a 9,557-ton tanker from Liverpool, was as good as dead. The boarding party came back in two boats, with forty English captives, several of them wounded, and the word that the captain had died on his bridge, and three others were missing.

In spite of the word that another ship had sent the message the second time, Captain Rogge asked the radio operators why they had sent the distress calls after asking for medical assistance, which meant they had surrendered.

"We didn't," said the radio operators, but they offered the

idea that perhaps Captain Tomkins had done so after they left the radio room.

So *Athelking* was destroyed, the raider using 91 shells in all, up to the moment when the stern went down. Her bow stuck up incongruously out of the water until the tanks were riddled by machine-gun bullets and the ship slid beneath the waves.

The whole affair had consumed three and a half hours, from sighting to sinking.

Once again *Raider 16* had marred the record of humane action, but the captain did not learn the true story immediately. Nor did he have time to do more than speculate that Wenzel was right—another ship had repeated the distress call—for he must get out of that vicinity.

The raider's radio operators were picking up strange signals addressed GBXZ—which meant To all British Warships, and he could assume that they referred to the distress call of *Athelking*. Captain Rogge headed north and east to cross the 20th parallel almost directly in line with the southern tip of the Indian peninsula.

The captain was not entirely pleased with recent events. The old days of the gallant *guerre de course* were irretrievably lost to the days of high-speed radio. War had become a business of killing.

CHAPTER THIRTEEN

The Airplane

Flying Officer Bulla was probably the most disconsolate man aboard *Raider 16* in the early summer of 1940, because very quickly in the game his HE 114 had literally fallen apart, and he was in the position of being an airman afloat, which is to say as much in distress as a sailor away from the sea.

Early in August, Bulla and the aircraft mechanics aboard the raider had pulled apart the crates in which were packed parts for the seaplane. They worked day and night for four and a half days, and finally assembled a new aircraft. It was not exactly an HE 114, because they had no written instructions, but they put together an airplane and it flew.

Captain Rogge had to admire the persistence of his airmen, although privately he believed the HE 114 to be inferior to the World War I airplane used by the raider *Wolf* in her peregrinations. Reluctantly, and as long as it did not detract from the business at hand, he gave permission to Bulla to carry out a few practice flights. First the pilot took off with 45 gallons of gasoline and nothing else aboard, and made a shaky sweep around the ship before landing. That same day, the crew mounted the 20 mm. cannon and a pair of 110-pound bombs on the seaplane, and she still flew satisfactorily.

Next attempt at resurrecting the aircraft as a useful device had come during the encounter with the *Talleyrand*. A few hours after the first flight, Captain Rogge thought that perhaps the airplane could be used to destroy the radio aerial of a ship by shooting and bombing, and once it was decided that *Talleyrand* would be consigned to the deep, this procedure was given a try. Bulla took the plane off in the calm sea that afternoon and tried the radio trick. It did not work, but he did have more success in shooting up the bridge and the radio operator's cabin, and this little victory led Captain Rogge to believe it was worthwhile using the plane in an attempt to make a ship stop without sending out a distress signal.

So with this background, when on September 10 at high noon the lookouts in the mastheads of the raider reported smoke on the port quarter, Captain Rogge sent for Flying Officer Bulla before the alarm bells had stopped ringing.

Was Bulla ready to try to work out on a live target?

He was.

The HE 114 was put over the side, loaded with 60 gallons of gasoline, two 110-pound bombs, and 120 rounds of 20 mm. ammunition for the cannon. A grapnel was fixed to a line; Bulla was to zoom in on the ship and try to catch her radio aerial (running between the masts) and rip it loose as he passed over.

Soon all was ready, and then Captain Rogge called Bulla back to the bridge.

"Listen," the captain said. "I have an idea. We will try to launch your plane during a rain squall . . ."

The idea came from a chance conversation with the Asian prisoners, who had admitted that they hated loud noises aboard ship, and that the men below always panicked at the sound of gunfire.

Rogge's sharp mind had taken the matter further, and now he laid out his plan to his flying officer. Bulla would fly out of the squall to give him a chance to sneak in on the other ship. He would try his aerial grapnel trick, but above all he was to shoot up the bridge and funnel. Who knew, by shooting up the funnel he might reduce the ship's draft enough to bring the boiler pressure down and stop her. By shooting up the ship at all, he would create enough racket to frighten the stokers, and perhaps bring them up from below. And finally, by making several shooting passes at the bridge and funnel, Bulla would distract the officers on the bridge so that they might not observe the advance of the raider toward them.

Certainly it was worth trying. Bulla would start shooting and Rogge would bring up *Raider 16* at full speed.

At this point the other ship was about 18 miles away, scarcely more than a handful of mast sticks and tall funnels. Navigator

Kamenz noted that they were on converging courses—which was enough for the moment.

For a time haze obscured the other ship, but then it lifted. For a time, also, the other ship altered course away from *Raider 16*, as it had been specified to merchant captains by the British Admiralty to avoid raiders; but Rogge played a cat and mouse game, turning toward the other ship's course when she was over the horizon, then turning away from her when he saw her come up again—as if he, too, was trying to avoid contact with another ship that might be an enemy.

After a time a squall came up, and Rogge turned to port and launched the seaplane. It stood in the lee of the raider for a moment, then began to move along the choppy water and took off safely.

As the plane flashed overhead and toward the enemy, Captain Rogge ordered full speed ahead and turned directly toward the ship he was intent on capturing.

"QQQQ . . . QQQQ . . . QQQQ . . ." came the call, intercepted in Radio Officer Wenzel's shack behind the bridge, and then a position was given—which was some 60 miles off the position the ship actually occupied.

In five minutes Bulla was zooming in to attack the other ship, battering her bridge and funnel with his 20 mm. cannon, dropping low to try to pick up that radio aerial with his grapnel. He attacked for 22 minutes, dropped his bombs, and expended his ammunition, then came back alongside *Raider 16*, radioing the course and speed of the other ship.

Bulla expected to be picked up, but Captain Rogge had no time for him at the moment. The airplane landed, but by the time it was stopped in the water *Raider 16* had sped past, on her way to attack.

Rogge headed toward the position indicated, but all he saw ahead was a rain squall. Through it, seven long minutes after hearing from Bulla, the raider found the other ship, back on her old course, with not a soul visible on deck or at the rear gun.

The raider hoisted her German naval ensign and the flag ordering the other to heave to. The camouflage was dropped away from the guns.

Rogge ordered a pair of rounds fired ahead of the ship. They splashed in the sea well forward of the bow—but brought no signal nor any sign of life. Kasch fired a salvo across the bridge. Still nothing. It was as though the ship had been deserted.

Ten minutes passed before the ship began to lose way and finally came to a stop—minutes in which Rogge was of two minds, to sink her right then or to save her as a possible prize and to search for papers. For although he had the British merchant codes, the enemy had gathered as much (that someone was breaching security) and had begun to change the code usage. Without new information, the codes could no longer be properly deciphered.

When the merchantman came to a stop, Rogge sent his boarders over. Seeing the boat coming, someone on board the merchant ship began sending again:

"QQQQ . . . QQQQ . . . QQQQ . . . SS *Benarty* bombed by plane from ship . . ."

So that was her name—*Benarty*. But why was she signaling? How could one account for her erratic course of action?

"Put a shot into her bridge," ordered the furious Rogge when he heard the radio. His anger was always aroused when a ship apparently captured turned on him and tried to bring on the cruiser or other enemy he feared so much.

"*Feuer!*" shouted Oberleutnant Kasch to the forward starboard gun, and a shell went screaming through the air, to land in No. 3 hatch abaft the bridge, hurling the hatch cover aloft and starting a fire in the hold.

The British crew began running for the boats. Captain Rogge ordered the signalmen to tell the boarding party to put out the fire if possible.

So the boarding party went to work. The captain and the chief engineer were taken back aboard the *Benarty*. There the Germans discovered that the engine telegraphs were set at full speed ahead—the reason the ship lost steam was that the stokers had, indeed, abandoned their posts when the ship came under air attack.

And so the airplane had proved itself. It was a valuable weapon in this business of killing, after all.

CHAPTER FOURTEEN

September Blues

The *Benarty* had much to tell Captain Rogge and his men about the war at sea in those days of September, 1940. She was a 5,800-ton freighter, built in Glasgow in 1926, hardly a likely repository for His Majesty's important Admiralty mail—but that is what she was carrying. Adjutant Mohr, in his usual efficient fashion, went aboard and rummaged through the wastepaper baskets. But besides these papers he picked up sackfuls of official documents which were taken back to the raider for study.

There were some more cipher tables, and messages, which made it possible for Radio Officer Wenzel to decipher the reciphered codes. Some of the material was also sent off by radio to the cryptologists in Berlin, and they completed the job. So for the next few days—until the British reciphered the codes again—the merchant vessels could be kept track of by their messages.

Mohr learned much more. He was fascinated by a secret service report on a Mr. Hilton of Rangoon, who was suspected of spying for the Japanese in Burma—Mrs. Hilton was the Irish lady who had been friendly to the Germans. Much was explained by the secret service report.

The adjutant also learned that *Benarty* had been the ship which, the day before, had rebroadcast the distress message sent out by *Athelking*, and had thus probably caused the death of Captain Tomkins when the Germans reopened fire at short range on the bridge of the surrendered ship.

And finally, Mohr learned that they had been hunting in the finest grounds of all, where three trade routes intersected at 22° South, 68° East. But that intersection obviously had become dangerous to them as well as deadly to the British—and it was time for them to move on.

Taking all this information, Captain Rogge again showed what made him a great raider commander: his ability to learn and adjust his tactics to the situation at hand.

He knew that the British Admiralty was aware of the existence of raiders in the Indian Ocean, although he had neither been identified nor pinpointed, and he learned from the captured material how the British were taking evasive action and maintaining guard. He had been able to approach *Benarty* only because he had pretended to turn away from her and thus had allayed her fears. So he learned that innocence was his best guise, and he laid plans to look more like a British ship than a neutral. (*Benarty* had taken *Raider 16* for a Greek.)

The idea now was to take the camouflage off the rear 150 mm. gun, which was almost 6 inches by British standards, and make the gun appear to be a British 4.7 inch, standard for merchant ship afterguns.

Also, because British ships were now cautioned to pick up and retransmit any distress signals from other vessels, Rogge vowed to have a slower trigger finger in the future. He was trying his level best to bring gallantry back to a war that brooked no gallantry. He was so particularly displeased with the events of the past few days that one might say the captain of *Raider 16* suffered from the September blues.

Matters were not helped much by an overlap in his raiding area with that of *Pinguin*. The fact was that each ship encroached a little on the territory of the other, and the German Admiralty became furious with Rogge and with Captain Ernst Krueder of *Pinguin* for duplication and for endangering one another. *Pinguin* was only some 700 miles away from *Raider 16*, south of Mauritius, when she should have returned to the Atlantic or into Australian waters. Caustic messages from Berlin did very little to make Rogge's temper or spirits better, and he decided to lie low for a time and await developments.

For a week after sinking *Benarty* the raider cruised in these waters, heading south, and then decided to move toward Australia. On September 19, Rogge ordered the engines stopped and the ship began to drift, to conserve fuel. She was drifting at 22:55 then when the port lookout on the bridge sighted a heavy smoke cloud on the quarter, which seemed to be steering west—possibly bound out from Australia for South Africa, or beyond.

Rogge sounded the alarm, and called for speed. But *Raider 16* had been drifting, and although she was a motorship and not a steamer which would have to get up steam in the boilers, she did have her limitations. If Rogge wanted full speed, he would also have to have a shower of sparks from the unconsumed oil in the cold fireboxes. Traveling at night, hunting, the captain did not appreciate a column of sparks rising above his ship, and so he had to content himself with 12 knots for half an hour while the engines and the fireboxes warmed up.

Rogge decided to circle around the other ship and come up from the rear, and allowed himself until midnight to make the maneuver. At 00:08, then, he was in position on the target, bearing 145 degrees, and at 5,000 yards. There was no indication that the raider had been sighted, so they dropped in closer, to 3,500 yards. Then Rogge saw that he was about to attack a passenger cargo ship, something he had no desire to do. He decided to try to capture her without a fight, and challenged.

"Heave to," flashed the signal lamp. "We are boarding."

"Understood," came the answer.

"Do not use your radio."

"Understood," came the answer. But she kept going.

"Heave to or I fire."

"Understood."

"What ship?"

"*Commissaire Ramel*."

"Await my boat."

"Understood."

So all was understood and all was settled. Or so it seemed. *Commissaire Ramel* stopped and blew off steam. She switched on her lights, and played captive as docilely as one might hope.

Raider 16 came in at 10 knots, slowly and carefully, but not on edge. It seemed an easy capture.

Then came word from Lieutenant Wenzel's radio room.

"Enemy transmitting!"

What was Rogge to do? He hesitated for a moment. She was a passenger ship—but she was also an enemy.

"*Krieg ist Krieg,*" he said. "*Feuerlaubnis!*"

So Gunnery Officer Kasch sent shells screaming into the enemy's side at almost point-blank range, and she began to burn.

The radio room of the raider began jamming the enemy's transmissions on the 600-meter band. Her radio went dead.

"*Halt, Batterie, halt*," shouted the captain of the raider.

"Transmitting again, on 18 meters," came the shout from the radio room.

"RRRR . . . RRRR . . . RRRR . . . *Commissaire Ramel* gunned . . ." was the call.

And now Lieutenant Wenzel reported that the distress call was being picked up by radio Mauritius and other shore stations and circulated across the Indian Ocean.

Rogge told Kasch to fire at will. Some 50 high explosive shells from the raider were sent into the burning ship, and fires lit up like a lighting system, blinking through the portholes. A sheet of flame arose on deck and spread across the length of the ship. Two boats dropped into the water, and a signal came from a light.

"Send a boat."

Although the sea was running high, Rogge did send a boat, but by the time the boarding party reached the other vessel, the flame and seas were in such condition that she could not be boarded. One of her own boats lay off the stern, while two others were drifting about in the darkness. The crew of one boat had stepped a mast and were making ready to sail away.

Why? Rogge could not understand why the boats did not come to the raider.

Mohr and his boarding crew were in the raider's boat, tossing up and down and trying to rescue the British seamen in the water. Fortunately, the seamen were wearing life jackets with lights attached, and one by one they were hauled into the raider's big motorboat.

Then one of the Germans saw a piece of wreckage floating on the surface.

"What's that?" he said.

Mohr said it looked like flotsam. But as they neared, they saw it was a small raft with a young boy clinging to it. They tried to help him into the boat. He resisted. Mohr saw his face: the boy was paralyzed with fear.

The raft slipped away but Mohr chased it and they dragged this fifteen-year-old cabin boy aboard, the youngster fighting them all the way.

"Don't kill me! Don't kill me!" he cried.

The boy believed that the Germans were saving him only to torture him, and the Germans of *Raider 16* did not realize that U-boats and other raiders had already abandoned many captives to the sea and had given the Allied and neutral sailors of the world good cause to fear for their lives.

In an hour the roundup was complete, and 42 Englishmen, 14 white and 7 black Frenchmen were brought to the deck of the raider. One Englishman and 2 blacks had been killed by shell-fire. So the rescued men went to join the other prisoners, while the flaming *Commissaire Ramel* was sent to the bottom in a cloud of steam and smoke. She had been a 10,000-ton ship carrying a mixed cargo from Australia to England.

Rogge was angry again. Someone had sent an SOS after surrendering, and this action had caused him to waste shells, sink a ship that he wanted to capture, and kept him from searching her for papers. He brought the English Captain MacKenzie to his cabin and began dressing him down, to learn that the captain had been playing bridge in the saloon when the attack came, that he had rushed on deck, passing the radio shack, and had automatically ordered the operator to send an SOS before he knew that the French first mate had surrendered. So once again Rogge was faced with the vagaries of humanity in his attempts to carry out an orderly war in the tradition of the old *Emden*. Radio was the greatest nuisance of his war!

The raider had been operating successfully for some time in the vicinity of 70° East and 30° South, but with the sinking of *Commissaire Ramel*, Rogge saw that he was in mortal danger here. For weeks he had been teaching his officers to "think like the enemy." In the wardroom of the raider hung a huge chart of the Indian Ocean, and using this, Rogge gave chalk talks.

"Put yourself in the enemy's skin," he said. And he outlined how, if he were the admiral commanding in Colombo, he would begin searching the Indian Ocean for this raider. After *Commissaire Ramel* sent its SOS, the British admiral had on his position chart five points from which distress signals had been heard, and if he joined those positions with a line, he could figure very easily that a raider was working these waters. There was the additional confusion of *Pinguin* working the waters closely and that helped a little in the case of *Raider 16* but not that much, not enough to justify *Pinguin*'s invasion of *Raider 16*'s territory. The trouble was that at this time *Pinguin* was only 90 miles away and it was time to get out. So, on that early morning of September 20, Captain Rogge set a course to the northeast, which would take him out of the sea-lanes, in the general direction of the Cocos-Keeling Islands. The engines were giving trouble again and the chief engineer wanted promise of some down time so he could overhaul cylinders and exhaust valves and pistons, all of which were worse for wear.

The days went by slowly but gently. Rogge gave his chalk talks. Mohr held intelligence sessions for the officers, giving them information about the war in Europe as it came in over the radio. Berlin had made it a capital offense for a seaman or officer to listen to enemy broadcasts, but Mohr was the exception; it was part of his intelligence work to get word of the enemy, and sometimes he found the American and English broadcasts brought him more information than the propaganda reports that emanated from Berlin. Officers and crew also spent part of these quiet days altering the camouflage of *Raider 16* a little so she would appear to be a British auxiliary cruiser.

Thus the blues of September began to dissipate—until September 27. On that day they had word of the fate of *Tirranna*.

Their captive, their prize, had steamed around the Cape of Good Hope and up the South Atlantic, passing eight ships including a British cruiser without incident. She had moved in between Madeira and the Azores. *Raider 16* had gone to considerable trouble to be sure that Berlin was in touch with her—but Berlin had been calling *Tirranna* all the while on the wrong radio frequency, and so the captive never did receive her instructions. But she made the voyage safely anyhow, and anchored off Cap Le Ferret. Lieutenant Waldmann had sent Lieutenant Mund ashore to Arcachon to telephone Berlin and secure instructions, for he had gained the impression that St. Nazaire Harbor was mined. Berlin had then ordered the ship to steam to Bordeaux, not bothering to tell the lieutenant to take antisubmarine precautions. Next day, she was torpedoed by the British submarine *Tuna* off the Gironde. All but one of the prize crew members rescued themselves, but 60 prisoners were drowned, including women and children. Lost were cargo, mail, important papers, and reports from *Raider 16*.

September went out, bluer than ever.

CHAPTER FIFTEEN

The Tale of the Durmitor

Captain Rogge headed toward Sunda Strait, stopped in mid-passage for overhaul, and then started up again. He sent the seaplane out for a reconnaissance flight, to try to discover the route taken by ships moving out of the Strait. The plane was not working properly, it broke a strut on landing, and Rogge decided not to use it again for a while.

The first three weeks of October proved dull and tiresome. The crew began growing restless, the captives more so, and the restlessness of the prisoners communicated itself back to the crew. Much of the problem concerned the food. The Germans ate black bread. On Wednesdays they had curry. Other days they drank ersatz coffee in the morning and ate a hunk of bread and margarine. At the big meal at noon they had one course of peas, beans, lentils, or noodles with blood sausage or some other German preserved meat. Supper was like breakfast.

On Sundays they ate potato chips, canned vegetables and canned meat, or a stew. Water was short, each man received a quart a day for drinking and washing, and the taps were locked so that only the pumpmaster could issue the water.

Conditions were almost the same for Germans as for prisoners, and after seven months at sea the Germans were showing the strain. As for the prisoners, Captain Rogge was forced to take strong measures to keep them under control and once a prisoner had to be disciplined by the officers of the raider, as an example to the others.

Normally, discipline of the prisoners was in the hands of their own officers. The crew members messed and lived together under control of their officers. Orders were transmitted to the officers by the Germans and then to the men by the British and Norwegian officers.

One day an English seaman refused to obey an order from his own captain. The captain was embarrassed and was inclined to forget the matter, but a German had seen, and reported the matter to Adjutant Mohr. The man was brought to the adjutant's office.

"Why did you refuse to obey orders and insult your captain?"

"I'm not his servant," said the man. "We're all the same now. He's no better than me. No one can force me to fetch his property."

The incident was referred to Captain Rogge, and he ordered the man to the brig until he changed his mind. The English captain pleaded for leniency, but Rogge was firm. It was not a question of the captain's feelings. It was a matter of discipline. If others saw this man get away with disobedience to an order, they would try it. And if all the prisoners did it, the German sailors might try it. The idea was contagious, Rogge said.

It was action—action and nothing else—that eliminated the problems of boredom and discipline. Action came again to *Raider 16* on October 22 when she captured the Yugoslav freighter *Durmitor*, a 5,600-ton ship from Dubrovnik carrying a cargo of salt from Spain to Japan.

Durmitor had given up easily; not a ot was fired; and Rogge was so eager to get rid of his current batch of prisoners that he took a very narrow view of the prize regulations in this case. By using his radio (to ask the raider who she was) the captain of *Durmitor* had violated Article 39, Section 3, of the regulations: "Assistance given to the enemy by radio despite orders to remain silent." And because she had stopped off in Cardiff earlier, she was also accused of violating another article: "Carrying contraband via enemy ports."

There was no arguing with Captain Rogge once his mind was made up, and so *Durmitor* was captured.

After taking her, even Rogge was not so sure she was capable of the task he had in mind—use as a prisoner and official paper transport—but he had become quite discouraged recently with the incidence of use of radio by the brave British merchant captains, who would risk death and dismemberment to send those distress calls. Here was a chance to unload and he could not afford to pass it up.

Durmitor's hull was foul, so foul that she could barely make

7 knots. Her cargo weighed her down so the Plimsoll line was covered. She carried a crew of 37, only 15 tons of drinking water, 20 tons of washing water, and food for ten days. The Germans measured her coal and estimated it at 500 tons, enough to get her to Africa.

Rogge moved his prisoners aboard this old tramp. At first the prisoners were happy. They had been housed on the deck below the crew deck of *Raider 16*, where it was always as hot as an oven—and where the stink reminded one of the more educated prisoners of what he had read of the Black Hole of Calcutta.

Nearly 300 prisoners were to be shepherded across. There was no real place for them to sleep. They were to be herded forward and a barbed wire barrier set up. Behind it was a German machine gun mounted on the bridge, to be manned day and night. For sleeping, if the weather grew bad, the prisoners must go below onto the salt cargo. Only those over fifty years of age could have mattresses, and there was no other bedding.

Lieutenant Dehnel, one of the junior officers of *Raider 16*, was given a crew of fourteen to handle this ship and her prisoners, and he was sent off to rendezvous later with the raider, while she completed her operations in Sunda Strait and (hopefully) secured enough stores for the prisoners to take on their journey without cutting into *Raider 16*'s lean supplies.

So the raider moved into the Strait area. The weather grew hot and humid, and the crew began to act up, as Rogge had recently been afraid they would.

Three and a half weeks of heat and food shortage, water shortage and more heat, boredom and misery had told on the crew. Rogge knew that something must be done, or he might be faced with a mutiny. He recalled his conversations with Captain Nerger when the raider lay fitting in Hamburg—how Nerger had told him of the stringent measures he had taken in World War I to circumvent mutiny, not once, but several times. Rogge was determined not to let matters go so far on *Raider 16*.

The captain called the crew together and made a little speech. He was aware of the scuttlebutt, he said. There was a war, and they must stay at sea as long as possible. Thus rations had been reduced and might be reduced again. In fact, in this heat, less meat, fat, and butter was good for them.

If the men did not believe their captain, they had no time for complaint for he rushed on.

"The more privileges I grant you," he said, "the more I do for you, the more you ask for. We have been at sea now for seven months. The time has come to speak plainly before I have to take more drastic steps. I know that the heat makes us all slack, but cooler weather will bring cooler judgment. At all costs, the discipline of the ship must be maintained, for our lives depend upon it."

So the men were warned. Rogge then offered them a carrot on the stick. He would give each man an opportunity on a regular basis to have a week in sick bay "on leave" with no duties except at action stations. He would give them a free afternoon to "make and mend clothes" once a week. On hot days work schedules would be reduced. He would also try to find a deserted island where they could spend Christmas ashore.

Next day, October 26, they again met *Durmitor* at the rendezvous point, and if before Rogge had hesitated about sending his prisoners off in this old wreck of a ship, the atmosphere of near mutiny now made it certain that the prisoners must go to ease the strain on the raider. Two hundred and sixty souls were herded onto the foredeck, behind that barbed wire.

In the interim, Lieutenant Dehnel and his crew had pulled enough salt out of holds No. 1 and No. 2 to give the men room to stretch out. They had only tarpaulins for mattresses. They had a week's supply of bread from the raider's bakery. They had less than a quart of water per man per day for drinking and none at all for washing. *Durmitor*, then, was to be a hellship for the next three weeks. Nineteen days, the Germans said the voyage would last, but they told the prisoners it would be only two weeks.

Aboard went the 260 officers and men, to face a little demonstration from Lieutenant Dehnel. The sentries shouted for silence among the crowded, muttering men.

"Gentlemen," said Dehnel, "I've something to demonstrate."

He waved his hand.

The machine gun began firing, lashing the water ahead of the old ship with the lead of her bullets.

Captain Rogge had earlier asked all the merchant captains to give him their word that they would not attempt sabotage or mutiny and they had agreed. In view of Lieutenant Dehnel's exhibition, the captain's call for an honor system seemed supernumerary.

No sooner had the prisoners joined the ship than they learned of her deficiencies. She was infested with rats, roaches, and other animal life. Only one boiler was watertight. And almost as soon as the ship had moved out of sight of the raider, Lieutenant Dehnel discovered a hollow space beneath the top layer of coal—which meant she did not have the fuel to reach her destination, Mogadiscio in the Italian Somaliland. Dehnel had a new problem: if they were longer at sea, they would not have enough food. If he continued at 7 knots, they would run out of fuel. He reduced rations, reduced speed and, using the hatch cover tarpaulins, he raised sail to help drive the ship with the monsoon winds.

The prisoners found the salt chafed their skin and got into their cuts. They discovered the rats had burrowed under the salt and came out at night to harry them.

In a few days the water ration was reduced to one cup per man per day—and some of the prisoners began to tap the steam pipelines, drinking the hot rusty water. When the rains came the men cheered, and washed themselves and drank their fill for a few moments. But the rains disappeared as quickly as they came, leaving the open holds inches deep in watery salt, which brought running sores to the men who had to sleep on it.

The Germans lived almost as badly as the prisoners, and so did the Yugoslav crew, but the prisoners were nearly ready for rebellion until Dehnel took a delegation through the German mess, showed how they lived and what they, too, were eating.

The sails were not enough. The coal was not enough. Dehnel began burning everything that would ignite: barrels, hatch covers, furniture, doors, wooden paneling. He made briquettes of coal dust, sawdust, paint, and grease. He used anything that he could.

The nineteen-day voyage stretched out. The prisoners grumbled again. Dehnel patted his machine guns and pointed to a smoke cloud on the horizon. He did not know what it was, but he told the prisoners it was *Raider 16* and that all he need do was call her up and she would come and assist him—put the prisoners to death for mutiny if they budged.

The speed dropped to 3 knots.

The prisoners had been told (to keep them quiet) that they were being taken to neutral ground in Madagascar. But Second Officer MacLeod of the *Kemmendine* had occupied time aboard the raider in making a rude wooden sextant, and using that instrument he was able to tell his fellows that they were not heading for Madagascar, but north, and he guessed that the Germans were taking them to Italian Somaliland where they would be interned as prisoners of war for the duration. But what could be done?

They moved on, slow as tortoises in the hot Indian Ocean sun. Dehnel made fuel from everything, and the stench of burning paint hung over the ship, along with the sharp odor of the salt. For a time Dehnel thought he was going to make Mogadiscio, but then he learned by radio that British cruisers were shelling the port, and he turned away. On November 22, the *Durmitor* turned into the tiny port of Warsheik. On shore he could see a quay and a cluster of white houses with red tile roofs nestled under palm trees against a sandy beach. He signaled for a pilot, and signaled again. No answer. A third signal brought no answer. He waited. He waited all day, and finally at four o'clock in the afternoon, he decided to take the ship in himself. Five minutes later she was fast aground on a coral reef.

Out came the Italians to capture these foreigners. They took them in and marched them through the city to show the natives that the Italian army was not to be trifled with. It was hours and hours before Dehnel could find someone who spoke any language other than Italian or native, and could explain to him that they were Germans with their prisoners, and that Il Duce would not appreciate this treatment of the representatives of the gallant German ally.

Eventually Lieutenant Dehnel got a pilot and help, and the *Durmitor* was refloated on the tide and anchored so the prisoners could be brought back aboard. Also some supplies were brought aboard. They were sorely needed, for the Germans had come in with 440 pounds of coal left in the bunkers, 650 pounds of beans in the larder and not a drop of fresh water to cook them in.

Lieutenant Dehnel did sail to Mogadiscio, but the Italians brushed him away. Please, they said, would he leave immediately if not sooner? His presence in the harbor might bring the accursed British warships back.

So with a little more food and a little more water, Lieutenant Dehnel sailed into the port of Kismayu, dropped off his ship and his prisoners, consigned his mails to the German representatives there for delivery to the Admiralty in Berlin, and shook the salt of the "hellship" from his feet. Neither he nor anyone else connected with *Durmitor* would ever forget that voyage!

CHAPTER SIXTEEN

The Thirteenth Ship

It was more than a week after getting rid of the prisoners before *Raider 16* went into action again—a fortunate and uneventful period in which Captain Rogge could try to bring up the morale of his men by keeping the promises he had made to them. Freed of the burden of prisoners on his supplies, he could better the rations. Freed of the need for guards, he could give the men leisure. Even the heat and smell of the ship seemed better, once half the complement was eliminated. Rogge had not been pleased to send off the prisoners on that old hulk, *Durmitor*, and he wrote in his official reports that she was totally unsuitable for a prisoner of war ship, and that "it was necessary to disregard humane considerations." Given Rogge's personal commitments, there was the mark of a commander—if it became necessary to violate his conscience in behalf of his duty to his ship and government, his conscience must bear that greater burden. Fortunately, he learned later, although many grew sick and there was much trouble on the voyage of the *Durmitor*, no one died from the ill-treatment.

No, the life of a raider captain did not go well with that of a man of gallantry.

The Sunda Strait had proved to be no place to find ships, and on November 1, Captain Rogge had headed northwest for the shipping routes that led into the Bay of Bengal, to a point about halfway between the Nicobar Islands and the east coast of Ceylon. On the night of November 8, a day's run north of the equator, on the Colombo-Singapore route, Captain Rogge's lookouts sighted a smoke cloud against the lightness of the sky. *Raider 16* luckily was not silhouetted, for she stood against the dark horizon away from the sun, and was banked by heavy rain clouds. So Rogge was able to make a quiet swift approach without frightening his game.

Raider 16 lifted her camouflaged gunports on signal, and the men prepared to do the job they knew so well. But Rogge did not want to shoot—he hated the destruction of a ship that might be a prize valuable to his government, and he wanted to capture the ship, then make the decision about her fate.

So this time the German captain had adopted a new strategy and he would try it.

At 500 yards the searchlight of *Raider 16* blazed out, blinding those on the bridge of the other vessel. Her gun was not manned—a good sign that Rogge had a chance of accomplishing his aim.

"Heave to," came the order from the raider. "Do not use your radio. Who are you?"

"*Teddy*. Oslo. What do you want?"

"We will search you."

"OK."

"*Funkverbot!* Do not radio."

There was a silence. Then the ship signaled.

"May we proceed?"

"No. Wait for my boat."

"Who are you?" asked the Norwegian.

"HMS *Antenor*," lied the raider's signalman. (*Antenor* was a British auxiliary cruiser.)

The tanker—for that is what she was—blew three long blasts on her whistle to show that she was stopped. Adjutant Mohr and the boarding party set out to do what they had done so many times before. The searchlight men kept that light blazing on the bridge, so the officers could not see the approach of the German boarding party, and the Germans were on the Norwegian's deck, Mausers in hand, before there was any question in the minds of the others that they might not be what they claimed.

So *Teddy* was captured without a shot being fired.

Much, much better, from Captain Rogge's point of view.

Teddy, he discovered, was carrying 10,000 tons of fuel oil from Abadan to Singapore. What a marvelous prize! She also had 500 tons of diesel fuel aboard—which might come in very handy for *Raider 16*. But this was no time or place to worry about what was to be done with the prize—they were in the middle of the British lake and they had best move out of the lanes of communication. So Lieutenant Breuers, one of the young officers, was put aboard the *Teddy* with a prize crew, given instructions about a rendezvous, and sent off 500 miles to the south where he ought to find open water and safety in which to wait for *Raider 16*'s convenience.

Five hundred tons of diesel oil. That was something for Rogge to conjure with—it meant another two months' free movement in the Indian Ocean. He could think happily on that while he was making this planned sortie into the Bay of Bengal to see just what might be found there.

Now, the seaplane was put into use again. Rickety as it had become, it still could serve a useful purpose in scouting sea-lanes for ships, and on November 10 that is what Flying Officer Bulla did. He was successful, sighting an eastbound ship far to the north of them—one they would never have encountered without those eyes in the air.

Rogge set course to bring up with the other ship after dark, and in the moonrise that night he came up on this ship, another tanker. He hoped again to take her without a struggle.

But this time the tanker could see *Raider 16* in the moonlight—and having a ship come out of the gloom at full speed toward one was enough to cause the captain of the tanker to act.

Her radio began to sputter:

"QQQQ . . . QQQQ . . . QQQQ . . . Position 2° 34′ North, 70° 56′ East, *Ole Jacob* . . . Unknown ship has turned now coming after us . . ."

So the message went out into the air.

Captain Rogge faced his old dilemma. Another tanker. If he fired, she would go up in flames and the most he could do was rescue another crew to eat him out of his supplies and gnaw at his men's morale. He did not want to begin shooting until he found out what was in those tanks—perhaps it was a whole cargo of diesel fuel, enough to keep him out for months and months.

So he would again follow a policy of deceit rather than force. *Raider 16*'s signal lamps began to flicker.

"HMS *Antenor* here," the signal said.

"Please stop following me," said the other.

"British warship *Antenor*."

"No."

Raider 16 gave another call sign.

Finally the other ship answered, "Norwegian tanker."

"Please stop," said the raider. "I wish to search you."

"Understand."

"HMS *Antenor* here," Rogge said comfortingly.

"*Ole Jacob*. OK, stopped."

So the Norwegian heaved to. But her captain was no fool. The radio transmissions continued.

"QQQQ . . . QQQQ . . . QQQQ. Stopped by unknown ship . . ."

The signal was repeated several times on one frequency, and then on another.

Captain Rogge was angry, but he was not going to start shooting unless it became necessary.

He ordered the helmsman to move in close to the *Ole Jacob*. The motorboat hung in the davits, and Adjutant Mohr and Navigator Kamenz were in it already, along with a ten-man crew armed with submachine guns, pistols, and hand grenades. Mohr was dressed in a British naval officer's jacket and cap on top of his German uniform, so as to deceive the enemy as long as possible. Two men stood beside them, but the other eight men were under a tarpaulin.

It was a calm night with the sea moving in the long swell that rolled up from the south. As the ships came together Rogge could see the men on the bridge. He ordered the searchlight switched on, and it swept the stern, where the gun crew stood at their guns, wearing their low round British-style steel helmets. The light turned to the bridge, to blind the captain and his officers.

With a call of "Good luck," the boarding party boat was lowered into the water, the motor spat and started and Adjutant Mohr was on his way.

The silence seemed endless and ominous, for Mohr knew that the others were suspicious of this boat. They came alongside, and looked for *Ole Jacob*'s ladder. None was there.

"Are you British?" came the hail from the bridge.

Mohr shouted something unintelligible and it was lost in the scraping of the boat against the hull of the ship. Mohr gauged his seas, and on the rise of the swell he leaped to the lower chain rail, grabbed on, and pulled himself up. He stood there, then, on the deck, faced by a hostile crowd, some of whom were holding rifles in their hands. Immediately he pulled a German officer's cap out and clapped it on his head, wrested a rifle from the hands of a seaman and threw it over the side, and as his men came up with their machine guns and grenades he shouted, "I am a German officer. Hands up!"

For a second or two it was touch and go. For as Mohr said the words, he smelled the strong odor of high test gasoline, and he knew that the same thought was racing through the Norwegian captain's mind: a fire fight would mean an awful explosion and probably the end of every man on board the tanker. The Norwegians surrendered.

So Captain Rogge's ruse worked again, although this time he had really been pressing his luck.

Mohr went quickly to his work.

"Tanker *Ole Jacob* with 10,000 tons of aviation gas," he messaged. "Am cancelling her QQQ signal."

(One of the deficiencies of the Germans was that they had not learned that the British distress signal was sent in groups of four, not three. In the excitement, however, this seems to have been overlooked, and by using the ship's own transmitter and key with its distinctive sound, Mohr convinced the ships and shore stations that the tanker had indeed made a mistake. Indeed, he also convinced Berlin, for later Berlin joked that so frightened were the British in the Indian Ocean that a Norwegian tanker had mistaken a British auxiliary cruiser in the Bay of Bengal for a German raider, although no German raiders were in the area. So much for Berlin.)

For the rest of the night Radio Colombo called fruitlessly for *Ole Jacob* but finally seemed to be satisfied when a trawler repeated both the QQQQ message and the cancellation. *Ole Jacob*—its captain and much of the crew aboard the raider, and the ship now manned by Germans—said nothing more at all.

When Captain Rogge learned what he had in *Ole Jacob*, he decided he must save her, because one did not blow up 10,000 tons of aviation gasoline if it could be put to some good use. Navigator Kamenz was placed in charge of the prize crew, and *Ole Jacob* was sent some 300 miles south, to a point near *Teddy*, to await the coming of *Raider 16*.

Next morning was Armistice Day. It began on a glassy sea, when a lookout sighted a thin smoke cloud on the horizon to the southwest. Since the courses were converging, Rogge made no change, but watched as the other ship came up. Soon he could tell through his glasses that she was a Blue Funnel liner—British. The range closed, until they were at 4,600 yards. Then up went the camouflage traps on the guns, up went the flags, and off went the warning shot.

Immediately the enemy ship began radioing for assistance.

"RRRR . . . *Automedon* . . ."

And that was all that got away. For Captain Rogge had no more patience in the matter of radio.

The jamming began.

"*Feuererlaubnis!*" came the command, and the high explosive shells began to do their grim duty.

The range was down to 2,000 yards as the shells began to hit. The first salvo struck the bridge. The next three salvos seemed to strike heavily amidships, sending up their gouts of smoke and flame. A man appeared near the ship's gun, and that was enough to bring three more salvos from the Germans.

The ship was quiet, very very quiet, and Adjutant Mohr led his boarding party across the glassy water.

"I'd seen some of them looking pretty bad," Mohr wrote later, "but *Automedon* was the worst. My first impression as I swung over her side was one of incredulity at the degree of havoc our shells had wreaked. *Automodon* rolled, and as she rolled a mass of broken hawsers and ropes rolled with her, jagged splinters of steel and rope sliding around my feet, and the escaping steam of her riddled pipes breaking an otherwise uncanny silence. Her funnel was full of holes, her stanchion posts were riddled with shell splinters, and the disintegrated timber of her radio cabin lay in a heap, smoldering on the shattered deck."

The captain's cabin and that of the first officer had been wrecked. Dead and wounded lay in pools of blood on the deck. Some of the wounded were groaning.

On what had been the bridge lay the body of the captain killed instantly. So had been all the other officers, except the first mate. One body lay in the entrance to the chart house, face half blown away. More had been killed and six badly wounded. (Two later died of their wounds.)

The bills of lading could not be found, so the boarders opened the hatches. They found a cargo of military and technical goods that Mohr valued at millions of marks or pounds or dollars, whatever one pleased. It included airplanes, cars, uniforms, microscopes, machinery, cameras, and medicines.

Since Berlin obviously did not know that *Raider 16* was in the Bay of Bengal, and since it was not in his orders to be there at all, Captain Rogge was a little nervous about staying long. He wanted to save some materiel; particularly food and the mail, which might tell the Germans much about the war effort.

Mohr went to work in the strong room and there found fifteen bags of secret government mail, which included decoding tables, fleet orders, and naval intelligence reports. He discovered something even more valuable in the chart room: a long narrow envelope in a green bag that was to be thrown over the side for sinking in case of trouble. It was an evaluation by the planning division of the British War Cabinet of the military strength of the British Empire in the Far East, including notes on the fortifications of Singapore.

Rogge was delighted with this find; he recognized immediately that it was worth sending a man back to Berlin to carry it personally, and he began to make his plans.

Meanwhile, aboard the *Automedon*, the indefatigable Leutnant Fehler was having a field day. Rogge had said to hurry up the work of moving stores, because he wanted to get out of this sea-lane as quickly as he could; but Fehler kept asking for permission to remain.

"Have discovered 550 cases of whiskey in No. 3 hold," came one message.

Rogge let him stay on to retrieve it.

Next came a message saying Fehler had discovered 2.5 million cigarettes in another hold.

Again he was allowed to delay.

So it was mid-afternoon before *Raider 16* took *Automedon* along and escorted her a few miles away to sink her. Down she went by the stern at 15:07, to become the thirteenth victim of *Raider 16*. Captain Rogge had now sunk or captured more than 93,000 tons of Allied shipping, and was on the way to surpassing the record of his idolized Captain von Mueller of the *Emden*.

CHAPTER SEVENTEEN

Hard Aground

During the late afternoon and evening of Armistice Day Lieutenant Wenzel's radio picked up a good deal of traffic relating to the *Automedon*, including a coded signal from her sister ship *Helenus*. In fact, it became a real "flap," as the navy men put it, because *Helenus* and Colombo quickly came to the conclusion that the incomplete SOS meant something desperate had happened to *Automedon*. *Helenus* was following a parallel course to *Raider 16* at this time and might have been taken quickly. But Captain Rogge was not informed, the opportunity passed—and indeed it might not have been such a great opportunity at that, for suddenly the whole area was aflame, as could be heard by the radio traffic from Colombo, and even Singapore, which was calling up the *Durmitor* without success.

Captain Rogge had two days to make his plans before he came up on *Teddy* on November 13. Now one of the German raiders assigned to this general area—*Orion* or *Raider 37*—burned fuel oil, and she might have made good use of *Teddy* as a supply ship that could keep her in operation for many, many months. But in planning the operations of its far-flung raiders, Berlin had made no provision for one ship to capture supplies for another, so this crosshatch was too complicated an idea for Rogge to attempt on his own. It would have involved a series of messages for *Orion*, all the dangers of radio transmission and possible exposure by the excellent British direction finder system, and endless confusion. Rogge had already seen how badly Berlin could bollix up the works in the mishandling of the orders to *Tirranna* from the Admiralty's end, and he was not about to set up more complications for his already dangerous life.

So *Teddy* was sunk with scuttling charges (after one false attempt) and *Raider 16* set off for her rendezvous with *Ole Jacob*. They took her diesel oil, leaving her enough to reach a Japanese port. That was where Rogge had decided to send her, to trade the aviation gasoline to the Japanese for stores for the raiders in the area, and to get Navigator Kamenz to Japan, whence he could make his way back to Germany to deliver these very important documents.

On November 16, *Ole Jacob* sailed for Kobe, carrying the Norwegian crew of *Teddy* as well as her own, and a German prize crew. She arrived in Kobe on December 6, and the trade was made, although the Japanese concealed the transaction by moving the ship to a neutral port. The trade was made for 11,000 tons of diesel oil, put at the disposal of the German naval attache at Tokyo, and a new airplane. Navigator Kamenz was dispatched to Vladivostok, and then across the trans-Siberian railroad to Moscow and Berlin. He dropped off copies of the British war plans in Tokyo but could not be sure what use the Japanese would make of them, because they were so very important the Japanese authorities tended to believe they were forgeries planted just to confuse them.

Also on November 16, Captain Rogge set out for the south. For several days he and Kamenz and Mohr had been studying charts and handbooks of the sea, to try to find a proper place to land and stay. *Raider 16* needed some more work on her engines and the men needed a chance to get off ship and away from one another for a little while. Rogge had promised them such a respite. Now, when the Bay of Bengal could be expected to come alive with British hunters, it was a very good time to take a break.

They considered Prince Edward Island in the south, but found it too foggy and remote. They considered St. Paul and Amsterdam islands, but found them too accessible, which meant the British might well decide to call there. Finally, they decided on Kerguelen Island, 50° South, because it was practically never visited by anyone for any purpose. Once the island had been used by whalers and sealers, but those days were long gone with the new developments in the fur and blubber industries. Kerguelen was excellent, too, in that it contained plenty of fresh water and *Raider 16* was badly in need of water, and there were any number of fjords and crooked bays in which they could hide from casual observers. Furthermore, not long before the war the German survey ship *Gazelle* had charted the island, and Rogge had excellent up-to-date material on it. They had found special charts and navigation guides to these southern islands aboard the Norwegian tanker *Teddy*.

South they went, south and west, cutting through their old hunting grounds, passing near the points where they had captured *Benarty*, *Athelking*, and *Tirranna*, southeast then, toward Kerguelen, until December 1, when a message intercepted from Berlin caused Rogge to make a sudden change of plan.

The message was for *Pinguin* (*Raider 33*) and it was followed by a message from *Raider 33* to Berlin. In the traffic, it became apparent that *Raider 33* was about to dispatch toward Germany a prize ship, the tanker *Storstadt* with 10,000 tons of diesel fuel. Captain Rogge was almost as short of diesel fuel as he was of water, and no better news could have come to his ears. Further, *Storstadt* would give him a chance to clear his ship of prisoners once again.

So important was this matter that even the cautious Rogge was willing to risk sending a radio message, and he did dispatch one to Berlin, asking that the tanker be sent to a certain grid square (Tulip) marked on the German naval charts. Berlin responded immediately and favorably, and a rendezvous was arranged with *Raider 33* for Sunday, December 8, at 34° 47' South, 59° 55' East. *Raider 16* turned completely around, headed northwest again, and reached the rendezvous point in plenty of time. There was *Raider 33*. Captain Ernst Krueder came aboard *Raider 16*, the champagne was broken out in the wardroom, the best food and beer were sent to the lower decks that day, games were played, songs sung, and sea stories swapped by officers and men alike, and the tension that had been building for 300 days was suddenly allayed by the sight of friends from home.

That evening, *Storstadt* arrived at the rendezvous and the work began. Refueling took the night. Next morning, Rogge went over to *Pinguin* to return the visit of Captain Krueder, and the task of moving the prisoners began. The day was made even better by the news from Berlin that Rogge had just been awarded the Knight's Cross of the Iron Cross. The celebrations began once again, and continued until it was time to part. Rogge went back aboard *Raider 16*, Captain Krueder signaled hope of a pleasant voyage, and *Raider 33* steamed off. As soon as the prisoners were transferred to *Storstadt*, 16 tons of water and food for sixty days were put aboard the tanker, two German sailors were assigned to help man her, and *Raider 16* sailed away, taking only three wounded Englishmen who could not be accommodated on the tanker. Rogge took the old precaution of setting a false course, so that if *Storstadt* were captured the prisoners could give only misinformation, and then headed southeast on his true course only after *Storstadt* had disappeared beyond the horizon.

More Iron Crosses had been awarded by Berlin, and on December 11 Captain Rogge held a formal ceremony, conferring them on selected members of the crew. The temperature dropped every day as they moved south. On December 8 it had been so hot the men had been wearing shorts and sun helmets only, but down it came, until on December 11 they came into the "roaring forties," and two days later the thermometer droped to 37°F. That day it began to blow, with the wind coming in from the west, bringing with it rain and a heavy sea.

As the ship approached Kerguelen, Adjutant Mohr put information on the bulletin boards to tell the men where they were going and what they could expect to see. The island and its islets had been discovered by Count Yves Joseph de Kerguélen-Trémarec in the frigate *Fortune*, in 1772, and he had sailed around them again the following year. Then Captain Cook was there on his third voyage around the world. Until 1873 the islands were sometimes inhabited by sealers and whalers, who found no trees and much interior marshland, and a mountain, Mount Ross, which is 5,600 feet high. What interested Captain Rogge most was the extensive waterfall system, for he hoped somehow to be able to fill up the tanks of the *Raider 16* with fresh water so that the ship could stay on her raiding for many months to come.

Steady steaming brought the raider to within sight of land on December 14, and at first glance it certainly lived up to its name: The Islands of Despair. For what appeared in the dull morning light was a long dark stretch of reef with the tops of the giant mountains sticking blackly into the clouds, and snow showing on their flanks.

The invaluable Adjutant Mohr led the landing party, disguised carefully as whalers in leather clothing and furs, and using a whaleboat captured from one of their Norwegian prey. They headed in for Port Couvreux, which had been a settlement of the French in years gone by. It might even be occupied at this time, and Captain Rogge must know its status before he moves the ship into the harbor.

If there were men on the island they must be subdued. If there was a radio station (God forbid) it must be silenced. For Rogge really was nearly desperate for fresh water. In times past the distilling plant could have helped out, but the distilling plant used coal, and Rogge was short of coal.

It was nine o'clock in the morning when action stations sounded aboard the raider and the landing party prepared to go ashore. Down went the anchor. Into the boat went Mohr and a quartermaster and eight men, submachine guns under the planks of their whaler, pistols concealed beneath their jackets, and potato masher grenades in their shirt fronts. If they found a British radio station they were to wreck it with their grenades, and, of course, the important thing was to wreck it *before* a telltale signal could be sent.

Slowly the whaleboat moved in to the granite shore and the rising hillside where not a single tree grew. Suddenly the quartermaster tensed.

"Something moving on the beach," he shouted to Mohr. Mohr strained his eyes and saw nothing. He ordered full speed into the beach and they raced in, ready for opposition. But there was nothing, no sound, no action.

They rounded a small cape and saw before them a valley leading down to the sea, with five huts at the foot of the hill, paint peeling from the decaying wood. One, with a big glassed-in porch, looked very much like an Alpine chalet.

The seaman in the bow suddenly reached for his machine gun and pointed it toward the shore. Sure enough—there was movement there. Then the boat came closer, the angle of light changed, and they could see what was moving. It was a big sea lion!

They jumped onto the land, and either ran from exuberance or wandered around, accustoming their feet and legs to the feel of solid surface instead of the yielding of boat and ship. They searched the fishing sheds at the wharf, rotting sheds with rusted and broken hinges and hasps, but sheds that reminded the men of humanity and home. They moved along the path to the houses, along a brook that fed down into the sea, past clumps of brown grass and little heaps of stones. They went to the big house with the veranda, kicked open the door, and found a room furnished with table, stove, two chairs, and a lamp hanging from the ceiling. On one wall hung a calendar of 1936, advertising the merits of Pernod with pictures of nearly naked girls. They looked in the cupboards and found bottles, many of them, but all empty. They found a half loaf of bread, at least three or four years old, but without a trace of mold and quite edible. They looked out the back and saw neat sheep fences, enclosing fields where the sheep and goats had been kept. On another side they found a sty which contained the mummified bodies of two dead pigs.

The Germans wondered what had happened to the man or men who had last inhabited this place. From the bread and the pigs, they deduced that some person or persons had been in the house when a ship approached, and driven by loneliness, that person or persons had begged the ship captain for escape from the wilderness, that the captain had taken him or them along, and in such haste that the pigs had not even been slaughtered but had been left to die.

Mohr and his men wandered around in these ghostly surroundings for half an hour, looking at the skeletons of boats, at the sheds, at the pictures of the girls, and the date November 18, 1936, which was the last one circled on the calendar. They found a kettle half filled with solidified whale oil. They found beds and preserves and a box of dynamite.

Finally Mohr gave his signalman a message.

"Settlement uninhabited. No trace of British."

Back came the answer from *Raider 16*.

"Return to ship."

They made their way slowly through the haze down to the rotting wharf and the whaleboat, and once back aboard began planning for a landing. The German ship *Gazelle* had surveyed the outer harbor, not the inner. They must bring the raider in through a channel like a bottleneck, some 500 feet wide.

So boats were sent in to make soundings and set buoys, and when this was done, Captain Rogge began to bring his ship inside through a field of surface seaweed.

The first two buoys were left to port. All was well. The echo sounder was turned on, to verify the findings of the leadmen who had gone in with the boats, and a leadman also stood at the bow of *Raider 16*, swinging his line and shouting out his findings. The echo sounder recorded 6.5 fathoms.

"Six and a half," shouted out the leadman.

"Six and a half, fair."

"Six and a half."

"Five fathoms . . ."

"Still five . . .

"STOP BOTH!"

And in seconds, engines stopped but still moving forward, *Raider 16* crunched aground.

How could it have happened? No one knew. And the problem right then was not to fix blame but to get off.

In a moment Captain Rogge was trying to free the ship. He moved both engines full astern, then tried half on one, half on the other, full on one, full on the other. Nothing happened. The ship crunched a little but did not move. And, conservative captain that he was, Rogge stopped his efforts to drag her off with force, waiting to find out how she lay and what had become the trouble, lest he tear the bottom out of her in trying to get free.

He had come 300 days safely through enemy waters to be stuck on a desert island!

CHAPTER EIGHTEEN

Merry Christmas!

Captain Rogge picked up the telephone and called the engine room.

"Any water coming in?"

"No sir," said Chief Engineer Kielhorn.

Rogge was pleased—for a few minutes. Then came a report from below that the drinking water in the forward tank tasted salty.

So he knew the keel plates of the double bottom had been breached, and some projection of rock had stuck into the forward fresh-water tanks, located in the bottom of the ship.

The next step was to discover exactly what had happened and what was holding the ship. Sounding lines were sent down. The sounders reported that the ship was resting on a small pinnacle like a sharp church spire, which the boats' crews had not encountered as they came in with their sounding lines and buoys the day before.

The damage control party checked the whole ship and reported that all oil tanks and holds were intact. The problem, then, was localized in that pinnacle which was holding them fast.

Rogge sent the ship's diver down to discover what he could. The diver came back to report that the forepeak and No. 1 tank in the double bottom had been holed, and that was all. The retractable minesweeping spar had been stove in five feet beyond its normal position and had penetrated several transverse bulkheads, and altogether this had caused leakage of salty sea water into the No. 1 fresh-water tank which held 82 tons of drinking water. Obviously, the damage must be repaired or they could not go back into action and remain any length of time, even if they could get off the rock that held them like a fishhook.

Faced with the total responsibility for his ship in this precarious condition, Captain Rogge decided that he must go down himself and see before deciding on any course at all. He knew nothing about diving, but after a few minutes of instruction, insisted on putting the globular helmet over his head, and sinking into the cold water.

He came up with a typical Rogge report. Affairs were bad enough, but not as bad as they might have been.

For thirty hours, then, the men of *Raider 16* sweated in the cold air to get their ship free. Rogge called for tide reports, and set up a tidemaster ashore, to synchronize the efforts of the men on the ship with the high water. He shifted weight to the stern. Out came 30 tons of sand, 30 tons of 75 and 150 mm. shells, 540 tons of oil, 50 tons of fresh water, and tons of provisions and other supplies.

What a job! Men cursed as they carried the big 100-pound shells, passing them in a human chain to get them aft. The sand ballast was brought out in buckets. Cables and chains were hauled aft from the boatswain's stores.

But the ship would not move.

They took her down by the stern 8.5 degrees. Still she would not move.

The captain climbed down into the flooded compartment himself and assisted in pumping the compartment dry with compressed air, so the damage could be assessed.

They tried for three days. What would happen to them if they could not get her off—aground on a desolate coast with only a few weeks' supply of food?

They laid the stern anchor out and brought the bowers amidships. Nothing happened. Demolition Officer Fehler suggested blowing the rock up. Rogge said it might blow the ship up, too. Someone else suggested jettisoning all the fuel forward. Rogge said he was not sure that would get them off the rock but it would certainly put them out of the war.

December 16 was the fourth day. Adjutant Mohr stood on the bridge in the early hours of the morning watch. They had just finished running the engines at full speed for 53 minutes, with no success. Rogge had gone to his cabin to catch a little sleep.

Mohr stared out into the cold night disconsolately, considering the miserable alternatives of living out the war on this rock eating seal meat, or being picked up and made a laughing stock, or becoming prisoners of war. Suddenly, he felt that the wind which had been blowing steadily was growing stronger, and it kicked into a gale. The ship's motion changed, the rock became a fulcrum, and she slid to starboard on it.

Mohr blew down the windpipe that led to the captain's cabin. The captain responded and Mohr told him what was happening.

"Good," said Rogge. "I'll be right up."

Up he came in a moment, ebullient as ever. In a few minutes the ship was alive again, with all men on deck, piped by the boatswain to run back and forth from starboard to port to help roll the ship from side to side in the heavy sea. Suddenly, at the height of the storm, the ship swung slowly around, lurched, cracked, and was free.

Now came a period almost as worrisome as that when they were on the rock.

Rogge began giving orders, to get them out of that narrow inlet and in deep water again for the night.

A man stood in the bows and another in the stern, each with lead lines, and they cast and sang out their findings alternately.

"Full ahead engines."

"Half ahead."

"Stop."

"Ten fathoms."

"Full ahead."

"Six fathoms."

"Half ahead."

The telegraph was handled by Mohr, and it rang and rang and rang again as he moved the handles in response to Rogge's orders. In the four hours of the watch he moved that handle more than 200 times, before they escaped the inlet and made their way into the safe waters of the outer bay.

And then it was done, and the relieving officer of the watch came up to take Mohr's place.

This officer had slept like a baby through the whole struggle.

And at breakfast the others were even too tired to chaff him about it, for, as Rogge said, the relief was unspeakable—and for the captain most of all, for Berlin would never have forgiven his wrecking his ship by running aground, no matter if he had

Captain Rogge and a group of his officers

In one of its disguises, the 5.9 inch gun is made to look like industrial machinery being shipped to the Philippines

Survivors from one of Raider 16's victims are brought alongside

A British captive, 71 years old, tells of being captured during World War I by the *Emden*

One of Raider 16's victims sinks: *ZamZam*

Captains captured from several different vessels kill time on the
deck of Raider 16

Raider 16 refuels from a captured Norwegian tanker

A secret port, the Kerguelens, where Raider 16 had a peaceful
harbor and re-supplied with water

In the Indian Ocean, Raider 16 rendezvouses with another raider, *Scheer*

After Raider 16 is sunk, the crew heads home on board a U-Boat

Home at last, the exhausted survivors gather around Captain Rogge

sunk 200,000 tons of enemy shipping by this time instead of nearly 100,000 tons.

Of course, they were not out of it. There were repairs to be made, and the problem of securing fresh water must be surmounted. But in the flush of victory over the spear of rock, the men of the raider felt they could do anything at all, and were willing to try.

Soon *Raider 16* was brought into a secluded creek surrounded by 300-foot cliffs, with an entrance 600 feet wide, and almost hidden from the seaward side by the Jachmann peninsula. Here the repairs were to be made, the engines overhauled, and the fresh water taken aboard if they could manage it.

They needed 1,000 tons, that was the problem.

The captain and Mohr and Fehler went ashore and found a waterfall at the top of their cliff. There was the water. The problem was to pipe it aboard. It would take 1,000 yards of fire hose, and no one had ever measured the hose to see if there was enough aboard the ship. The idea was to use the waterfall as a water tower. Fehler, the demolitions man, talked about blowing something up, but Rogge shushed that idea quickly enough, and Fehler came up with the idea of capturing the water in a barrel with a hole in it and sending it down through the fire hose.

Well and good, if it worked.

The barrel was cut and fitted and taken ashore. It was 300 yards from ship to shore, and 700 yards from shoreline to the waterfall, which was 25 feet wide. There was enough hose. It took three hours for the men to climb to the top of the cliff and the waterfall, with barrel and hose, but they made it, the barrel was lowered into position, held by ropes; and it worked. The water came spouting out the other end. The water tanks could be filled, and Fehler went off happily to hunt ducks with the blessings of his captain.

Next day began the work of putting the hose together for the job. There were new problems. The hose parted in a storm. Some piping had to be made out of sailcloth. But enough was put together, and the whole connected from waterfall to water tanks. Again it worked. All but the damaged water tank were filled in two days, and extra supplies were stored in barrels.

Captain Rogge had promised the men a respite from the dull routine of shipboard, but he could not give it to them until certain work had been done and certain precautions taken in behalf of the safety of all of them. Gunnery Officer Kasch had one trying job. He and his gunners climbed up the cliffs and painted numbers on them, each number representing a square on the artillery chart. The guns were then sighted to these numbers, with calculations noted on ship as to range and angle, wind, temperature, and air pressure. Signalmen were posted on the top of the cliffs with calibrated instruments. They could warn the ship immediately of the approach of any enemy and give the square in which he was coming—so *Raider 16* could fire over the cliffs without ever seeing the enemy.

Equally vital, and more time-consuming, was the task of repairing the ship without dockyard facilities. The hole in the bottom was 6 feet wide and 18 feet long! The steel plates had been torn and stuck out straight down from the hull. First they must be gotten off, and then the repairs made and the patching done.

Removing the plates was the job of an acetylene torch man, but the only man who was familiar with underwater work had been sent home on the *Tirranna*, since it had seemed almost inconceivable that his special services would be needed. The others of the welding crew did not know the techniques for underwater and could not keep the flame lit long enough to burn off the broken, jagged pieces of plate. So the divers went down, drilled holes in the jagged pieces, and then cables were fixed to the plates, which were broken off by pulling on the anchor winches.

Before the No. 1 water tank could be filled with fresh water it first had to be pumped out, and then the holes filled with cement under pressure. Four men climbed down into the narrow compartment and began the work. Two of the men went down after all was ready, the manhole cover was closed on top of them, the compressed air blown in, and they stayed down for two days until the concrete had hardened and the leak was secure.

Then leaks began to show up elsewhere.

But in the interim came Christmas. Leutnant Fehler organized the celebration, which meant that no stone went unturned—or unexploded—so to speak. He set men to work making decorations, other men to work building Christmas trees in a treeless land, using broomsticks and bits of rope bound with wire and painted green.

On Christmas Day there was a great party. The men dressed up in their best blues, and Captain Rogge and his officers donned their dress uniforms. Cloths were on the tables, along with parcels wrapped carefully by the Christmas committee, parcels for every man, consisting of shoes and pencils, cigarettes, chocolate, and other delicacies and useful items, things taken for the most part from the ships the raider had seized or sunk. There were candles and hymns and jolly Christmas songs. The officers ate Christmas dinner with the men. Nine hundred pints of punch were drunk, the best dinner possible was brought out, and the men enjoyed a certain degree of tranquillity as the snow came down to blanket the decks of *Raider 16*. And yet there were marring factors. Leading Seaman Herrmann was busy on Christmas Eve on a rope platform painting the funnel when suddenly during an engine inspection someone below started the diesels, Herrmann's life rope slipped in front of the exhaust, the rope burned, and he was thrown to the deck below.

He was rushed to the sick bay, and all possible was done to ease the pain of his two broken legs, but the accident put a damper on the Christmas celebrations. Further, that evening the other family men were talking about Herrmann's wife and children, and thinking about their own wives and children.

They had been out, away from home without letter or word of any kind, for nearly ten months. They were depressed, and in spite of the punch, morale was hard to raise. Merry Christmas? Perhaps.

CHAPTER NINETEEN

On to Battle

Christmas did not accomplish all it might have to raise morale aboard the raider, even though Captain Rogge did everything he could, including reading the story of the Nativity from the Gospel of St. Luke, and making a little speech about home and loved ones. There were greetings from Grand Admiral Raeder, the commander in chief of the German navy, and another fifteen Iron Crosses for the men. But a storm blew up that night, which meant part of the crew must get back to work, for it was a gale, and the ship must be secured beyond any doubt.

Next day the first group of 37 men was given two hours of shore leave—yes, just two hours, for that was all that could be spared. There was simply too much to be done for Captain Rogge to live up to what he had hoped to do for the men here, and what the men had come to expect. But war was war, and the captain could do nothing about it.

The exigencies of war were driven home to the men four days after Christmas, when Leading Seaman Herrmann died of his injuries in the fall from the funnel. He was buried on Kerguelen with full military honors.

Just too much to do and too little time.

Flying Officer Bulla, one would suspect, would have virtually nothing to do, since his airplane was an enemy-spotting device and here there was no enemy. But Rogge put Bulla to work mapping the islands. The repair parties found more leaks in the hull of *Raider 16*, where the double bottom frames had been forced inward. These took time and pains to repair. It was also necessary to change *Raider 16*'s camouflage, because all the activity of recent weeks had given her profile much too much

116

exposure to the world. The funnel was widened and the roof of the upper bridge was removed to give the impression of a much squatter superstructure. Captain Rogge was particularly concerned about the descriptions that would be given out by the crew of *Ole Jacob* once they reached British hands. The new model was the Norwegian merchant ship *Tamesis*, so new a vessel (built in 1939) that she did not appear in the registers and even her call sign was not generally known. (That last was a matter Rogge needed to rectify with Berlin because the British would certainly know her call sign. He sent off messages to that end while the ship lay in Gazelle Bay.) Rogge was also carrying on other conversations with Berlin. He was criticized for sinking *Teddy* and her oil cargo rather than sending it to Japan or out for the use of other raiders. He was also criticized for being in the Bay of Bengal at all since his orders did not call for it—but Rogge had taken the position that since *Pinguin* was encroaching on his territory, *Raider 16* would do a little encroaching herself. At this time, Rogge also informed Berlin of the damage to the ship's hull, but asked for permission to remain in the Indian Ocean or go to Japan for ship repairs.

In the meantime the repairs continued, while the men in their two-hour shifts went wandering among the rocks of Kerguelen, seeking rabbits for *Hasenpfeffer*, ducks, and Kerguelen cabbage, to supplement a diet that had long since ceased to contain fresh vegetables.

Because he was unable to live up to his promises, Captain Rogge devoted extra attention to the little ways in which he expected to keep the men industrious and thoughtful, if not exactly happy. The ship had been fitted with many amenities in the beginning. It had comfortable quarters, sufficient showers and washbasins, good locker space and a reading room, as well as a library, barber shop, shoemaker, tailor, laundry, pressing shop, and a soda fountain. The library had been augmented as they went along with their captures, although books in English, Norwegian, and Serbian were of interest only to a minority of readers. Rogge had established a directorate of educational programs, hobby equipment, and games. Many ships had such facilities, better or worse than those of *Raider 16*. With 350 men now going into their eleventh month without seeing port, more was going be needed.

The enemy was boredom, and the antidote was activity, so

the activity was increased. Rogge made it a point to be available to any man any hour of the day, except when actually involved in operations. The "leaves" program was stringently observed, a man resting on a chair on the afterdeck might have a sign on his chair which said: "I'm on leave." If so, he was to be let strictly alone, no matter what the detail. Only a call to General Quarters could disturb him.

So the enemy was counteracted, and in a sense the very business of the crew these days helped drive away boredom. All but the sea lawyers could understand that no one had willed the raider to go aground, and that on their joint efforts would depend the degree of probability of their seeing home again. At night they sat around the big recreation room singing, ending up with the Brahms *Berceuse*.

"Good evening, good night . . . Tomorrow morning, God willing, you will awake to a new day . . ."

And the phrase "God willing" never failed to mean something special to this raider crew.

New Year's Day was celebrated, again helping a bit to bring up morale. But what would really bring morale higher began again on January 10, and that was action. The raider sailed from Kerguelen that day, steering north. The request to return to the old hunting grounds had been denied by the Admiralty. Rogge had an alternative plan: he would go to the Arabian Sea and raid there. He had talked this idea over with Captain Krueder of the *Pinguin* at their meeting, and it seemed an admirable idea, because in capturing the *Automedon* Rogge had discovered the wartime shipping routes laid out carefully on secret charts of the area.

They went cautiously at first, starting at 7 knots, and when the ship responded without a leak or a whisper, taking her up slowly to 9. Nothing happened. That night Rogge ordered Oberleutnant Kasch to fire a broadside—and sent men below to observe the effects of the vibration on their repairs. The repairs held, so later in the evening Rogge sent one of his rare messages to Berlin, stating that he was resuming operations.

Berlin was not very helpful, but to understand why, one must realize that the navy stood very low in the estimate of Adolf Hitler. Reichsmarschall Hermann Goering was completely jealous of his prerogatives as head of the air force, and would not provide the navy with proper aircraft (thus that HE 114).

Propaganda Minister Goebbels considered the German navy to be useful only as a propaganda device, and he was constantly throwing monkey wrenches into the strategic works, as he did now.

Much to Captain Rogge's disgust, on January 18 Goebbels' people broadcast a propaganda report scoffing at the British, and particularly the British navy, for failing to prevent the operations of "a single commerce raider." Aside from the untruthfulness of the report (the *Graf Spee* was resting on the bottom of the River Plate), the propaganda could have no effect abroad except to arouse the British to more activity against the raiders, and if there was anything *Raider 16* did not need, it was a half-dozen enemy cruisers with which to play hide-and-seek.

But Berlin's chairborne naval commanders had different ideas too, and once again they chided Rogge for his failure to keep them constantly informed by radio. Rogge's concern about being caught by his own radio was highly exaggerated, said Berlin. Perhaps, said Rogge, and privately he continued on his own course of maintaining silence as long as possible.

On the afternoon of January 22, when nearly opposite the Seychelles Islands, although much further east, Captain Rogge's lookouts sighted a black smoke cloud, and he began an approach to what he hoped was a coal-burning merchantman, because a coal burner in 1941 was unlikely to be an auxiliary cruiser.

He approached cautiously, not wanting to frighten the other ship.

He also learned something this day. Gone was the old way, in which he could steam almost boldly up to a potential victim and then fire a shot and display his colors. In recent months some eight German commerce raiders had been operating in the far-flung waters of the world, and the warship *Admiral Scheer* had come out to sink merchantmen as well. The British Admiralty, hampered as it might be by a thousand demands on its men and ships, was not lying down. There was a war to be fought against naval forces, particularly those of Italy, but the business of tracking raiders and operating against them was anything but forgotten.

One problem for the British was that the activities of *Atlantis* (*Raider 16*) and *Pinguin* were being confused. Even so, those radio messages sent by their victims had aroused the British to action. On September 9 when *Athelking* reported she was being shelled, two British ships were ordered to that position, but by the time they reached the area *Raider 16* was gone. On October 7, the British cruiser *Neptune* had set out to check various southern islands and had called at Kerguelen. She found it deserted, reported that it would be an excellent place for a raider to hole up, and had gone away. Had she come two months later the story would have been very different.

With the capture of *Ole Jacob* the British had changed their whole approach to raider hunting. The East Indies Station adopted a policy of getting the fastest ships toward the last-known position of a raider or its victim, then making provision for protection of all shipping near that area, getting fuel to the area in case of an extended search, and getting air search out over the area.

With the capture of *Automedon* a special force was sent out after *Raider 16*, and a few days later when Rogge burned *Teddy* so brightly, the British saw the fires and searched harder for him. Only some bad British luck prevented an encounter.

When *Raider 16* moved into Kerguelen in December, the British had stepped up their activity in this operational area of the Indian Ocean. The cruiser *Colombo* and the armed merchant cruiser *Carthage* patrolled the northern approaches of the Mozambique Channel. Other cruisers were in the area, ready for action.

As for the ship that Captain Rogge was trailing this day, it behaved in an odd fashion, but one totally approved by the British Admiralty. The moment that the other ship sighted *Raider 16*, at a distance of 12 miles, she turned hard to starboard. Seeing this, Captain Rogge turned to port, hoping thus to persuade the other ship that he did not want anything to do with her.

When the first ship saw the raider turn away, she went back to her original course. The range had increased to 18 miles. Rogge turned his ship on a course parallel to the other ship. A daylight approach was out of the question this day, so the captain planned a night interception. At dusk he changed course to intercept the other ship and called for the men to go to action stations. The waiting began.

By rights, having changed to an intercept course, given the course and speed of the other ship all afternoon, *Raider 16* should have sighted her quarry an hour after dark. The darkness of the tropics came down, swift and black, and the hour passed—and there was no ship. The navigators began plotting alternate positions, but nothing brought the other ship into view, and so at last Captain Rogge reduced the ship to war watch condition—which meant half the crew could leave their action stations—and the night was spent gazing around a horizon that was completely dark and blank.

Rogge did not give up. He followed the presumed course of the other ship until daybreak, and then launched Bulla in the homemade HE 114. The pilot discovered the target ship 25 miles to the north, then returned and landed near the ship.

Captain Rogge had a new plan, which he now broached to his pilot. He asked Bulla to move in with the plane and his grappling hook with the sun behind him, and try to snag the other ship's aerial. He would attack with 20 mm. cannon and with his 110-pound bombs. It was to be the same basically as the last time, except this time the motor launch with spare bombs and shells would be lowered to act as his tender.

Could Bulla do it?

"Yes sir," he said. "Anyhow, I can try."

So the attack began.

Bulla did his part—did it magnificently, in fact.

Where he had never before been able to grasp a ship's aerial with his hook, this time he did, and tore it loose. But somehow, the ship managed to begin transmitting.

"QQQQ . . . QQQQ . . . QQQQ . . . *Mandasor*, bombed from raider . . ."

Every other time, the raider's monitors had been listening and had caught the attempts of ships to transmit their distress signals. This time, for some reason, Lieutenant Wenzel's men did not catch the call and it was repeated and repeated. Pilot Bulla reported the transmission, but the radio room of the ship did not pass Bulla's message on to the captain. Consequently, precious minutes went by and the other ship sent her message as she zigzagged to escape the plane.

Actually, it would not have made that much difference, for the ship—*Mandasor*—was not yet in range of *Raider 16*'s guns. But the air was alive with the telltale transmissions.

"QQQQ . . . QQQQ . . . QQQQ . . . *Mandasor* chased by raider and bombed. *Mandasor* chased and bombed by merchant ship raider . . ."

The noise was terrible, miserable, frightening, and must be put to an end.

Lieutenant Wenzel got to work.

The first thing to do was sent an "acknowledgment" from Colombo.

"RRRR understood," was the message.

"QQQQ . . . QQQQ," came back again. "QQQQ . . . QQQQ . . . QQQQ . . . Chased and bombed by merchant ship raider bombed by his aircraft destroyed aerial by line thrown from plane . . ."

This occasion was far and away the longest time that any victim of *Raider 16* had ever been allowed to remain on the air. But in five minutes, the raider was in range and turned hard to starboard to bring all guns to bear on the other ship. *Mandasor* kept running and transmitting, zigzagging to escape the guns.

One salvo followed another. The shells struck home. The ship began to burn. Soon she was burning so briskly that communications between her bow and stern could be carried on only by boat.

Adjutant Mohr and his men went over the side in their boat to the other ship, made the bridge, and collected papers as usual. *Mandasor*, they found, was a 5,100-ton ship on her way from Calcutta to England. She had valuable stores, especially food, for the raider, and they were quickly transferred. Her captain indicated the new state of affairs in these waters when questioned by Captain Rogge, too. The Englishman said that he heard in Calcutta that the raider which captured *Automedon* had run in very close, and that is why he had turned away from *Raider 16* the day before.

What he did not say, what he did not know, was that at the very moment the captains were talking in Rogge's pleasant curtained office, the British cruisers *Canberra*, *Leander*, *Sydney*, and *Colombo* were rushing to the scene of the struggle—or thought they were. But unfortunately, the excited radio operator and officers of the *Mandasor* had misstated their latitude in the message, and when the cruisers arrived in the search area there was no sign of ships or struggle.

All afternoon and early evening were spent moving the stores out of *Mandasor* into the raider, then the British vessel was scuttled by Fehler and his demolition crew. She went down in six minutes, leaving the surface awash with floating chests of tea—telltale markers had the British cruisers been guided to the right spot. *Raider 16* spent more time, in the dusk, searching for her airplane and its tender, and when they found it the airplane was half sunk. The plane had popped a float in making a landing in rough water, and then taxied a long way to find the motorboat, whose engine had gone dead. The wind swamped the burst float and the plane capsized. Could the airplane have been saved? Perhaps. But there was no time to worry about the damaged plane and so it was sunk by gunfire and *Raider 16* was soon on her way again, minus the effective new weapon she had developed.

For four days nothing was sighted, then a lookout saw a smoke cloud which turned out to be a three-funnel ship. Captain Rogge thought she might be the *Queen Mary*, but whatever she was he wanted no part of her. Such a large ship was likely to be escorted by a ship as large as a battle cruiser, and even the liner might have heavier armament than *Raider 16*. (The ship was not the *Queen Mary*, as it turned out, but the 22,000-ton liner *Strathaird*, working as a troop transport during the war.)

On the last day of January, 1941, *Raider 16* captured the 5,000-ton British freighter *Speybank*—just as easily as a child picks his toy ship off the wading pond. On the evening of January 31, the lookout sighted the masthead of the freighter, the gun flaps were opened, and the crew went to action stations. The raider came in from 23,000 yards at 14 knots, fired a salvo, turned on her powerful searchlights, and that was almost the end of it. After three salvos the other ship stopped; she did not use her radio or make any attempt to fight or get away. She had sent no distress signal, she was undamaged—she was perfect for Captain Rogge's needs, and the 17 white prisoners aboard her offered no problems at all. Her captain had thought the raider was a passenger ship whose navigator was not paying attention to his navigation and was about to signal her captain a sharp word or two when the guns began firing and the lights lit up the ship and the sea. *Speybank* had just sailed from Cochin on January 25 and was well stocked for a long voyage. Lieutenant Breuers and a prize crew of ten men took the ship to a rendezvous point on the edge of the Malha Bank (10° South, 63° East) and waited for the coming of *Raider 16* after she had done more of her deadly work. The total was mounting: with this capture the raider could say that she had paid her way by disrupting

Britain's orderly flow of goods and men across the Indian Ocean.

Speybank was sent away to the rendezvous point shortly after midnight on February 1, and the raider continued her lonely patrol off the East African coast, now northwest of the Seychelles. Next day, low on the horizon the lookouts of *Raider 16* sighted a Blue Funnel liner, and made ready to give chase. But the liner, the *Troilus*, was having no part of any ships in her vicinity, and she matched Rogge course change for course change, to stay away. All the while she sent messages.

"QQQQ . . . QQQQ . . . QQQQ . . . 0326 S 5235 E . . . *Troilus* suspicious."

Captain Rogge's radio men picked up the message and tried to jam but they were too far away.

The message was repeated.

And repeated.

It was sent nine times in all, before Rogge sensed that something unpleasant could be connected with this Blue Funnel liner and he gave her up as a bad job.

It was luck for *Raider 16* that Captain Rogge did not persist in his attempt to take the *Troilus*, for all his fears about the efficiency of radio would have been realized. That very day the British sent their Force K out from the coast of Italian Somaliland, not very far from the position given by *Troilus*. Force K consisted of the cruiser *Hawkins* (7.5-inch guns) and the aircraft fleet carrier *Formidable*. But when the force found *Troilus* safe and no sign of *Raider 16*, the ships turned away—giving the unknowing Captain Rogge his closest call yet.

CHAPTER TWENTY

Meeting
the Admiral Scheer

After the unsatisfactory encounter with *Troilus* Captain Rogge headed East, toward the coast where one war earlier the light German cruiser *Königsberg* had created so much trouble for the British. Then Rogge turned south, not wanting to move in too close to the coastline of Kenya and Uganda, where British warships might be lurking, waiting for just such as *Raider 16* to show its profile.

On February 2, Captain Rogge sighted and tracked a Norwegian tanker all day long, making a plan for a night attack. Taking a tanker was always a problem, particularly with those 150 mm. guns of his. It was hard to hit a ship "just a little bit," and yet any time a raider went after a tanker it must be that way or the cargo would go up in smoke.

Rogge and his men devised a new trick. They made a big sign to be hung over the side of the raider. Then, at night, when they came up alongside the tanker, they planned to heave over their sign so it hung down the ship's side, and through an elaborate system of floodlighting, to make the message unmistakable to the men of the other ship. The message?

"STOP. DON'T USE RADIO."

Raider 16 came up close to the tanker, and Rogge ordered the usual signs, the breaking out of the ensign, the flashing signal warning the other to heave to and not to radio, and the new sign so brightly floodlit.

"Don't fire into her," he said. "Rely on the sign and a shot."

Lieutenant Kasch repeated the order to his men—they were to fire over her, not at her.

"Feuer!" shouted Kasch.

"On lights," shouted Captain Rogge.

The lights came on, the floods and the searchlights, and they illuminated the effect of the first shot—it had gone straight into the funnel of the tanker.

"You lunatics," shouted Lieutenant Kasch to his gunners, "you've hit the funnel."

Before the firing could be stopped the German ship had fired three salvos, but luckily only the funnel had been damaged. The crew of the tanker milled about the decks with flashlights. The tanker's lights came on and she came to a stop. Two boats were hastily thrust over the side, so hastily that one of them capsized, and in a few moments there were a dozen bodies struggling at the stern of the tanker, someone flashing an SOS with his flashlight.

For both, victor and vanquished, it was a very disorderly performance.

"Away boat," shouted Adjutant Mohr, and he sped across the water to discover what was happening. Aboard the tanker he could not find the captain—he seemed to have completely disappeared. Finally the captain did appear, disoriented and thoroughly confused by the events. The crew, consisting of 9 Norwegians and 43 Chinese, was equally confused, and the Chinese, in particular, were milling about the deck, carrying bundles and shouting at one another. When Mohr approached one Chinese and demanded the name of the ship, that Oriental dropped his bundle and flung himself into the sea, from which he had to be plucked by the German boat crew.

Mohr made his way to the radio room and found the name and call sign pinned to the wall. She was the *Ketty Brovig*, he discovered. He ransacked the captain's cabin and found the manifest: 4,500 tons of diesel oil and 6,000 tons of other fuels.

The diesel oil would keep *Raider 16* in fuel for several months, so Captain Rogge decided that he would make an attempt to salvage the ship, although his gunners had wrecked her draft system. A shell had pierced the main steam pipe just above the main valve. The boilers had to be cooled before it could be repaired. This meant all the boiler water would be lost.

Mohr went back to investigate and confer with the chief engineer of the tanker.

How about running in fresh water after the boiler water was drained out?

"Impossible," said the engineer. This ship's boiler water feed pump and fuel pumps could be driven only by steam.

Well, how did they get steam up in harbor, if they could not start from scratch?

It had to be supplied from shore.

A most peculiar ship, said Mohr.

So the problem was to preserve a little bit of steam before it all escaped through that broken pipe and hope they could build it up from there. One of the Germans wrapped himself in blankets to protect himself from the escaping steam, climbed up to the main valve, and shut it off. The hissing slowed and died down as he turned the handle. The German stumbled back down to the deck, and the engine room was suddenly quiet.

That night the raider's engineers fabricated a metal jacket to fit the burst pipe and next day they put it on.

Lieutenant Fehler, in charge of the crew, was told to get up steam. The trouble was that the fires were out and one must have a hot fire to burn oil. So Leutnant Fehler, who loved to break things as well as blow them up, had a field day breaking up furniture and building a hot wooden fire to start the furnaces of *Ketty Brovig* once again.

At dawn, the ships parted company, Fehler to go to a rendezvous and wait until February 18; *Raider 16* to continue her depredations of the enemy sea-lanes.

Captain Rogge now had many new problems on his mind. He was no longer a ship commander but a fleet commodore, yet unlike the old days he must clear nearly every action with Berlin. So, unhappily, he risked a long radio message, explaining that he had captured the *Speybank* and wanted to send her home as a prize. He proposed to bring the ships together and fuel *Speybank* from *Ketty Brovig*, then transfer provisions back and forth as necessary before sending *Speybank* home to Germany. He also requested a meeting with *Kormoran* (*Raider 41*) and *Admiral Scheer*, the pocket battleship.

Admiral Scheer was supposed to have gone out raiding even before *Raider 16* moved out, but she had been undergoing a major machinery overhaul when the war broke out, and in the necessary changes of putting the navy to war, she was delayed for many months and was not ready for sea until the autumn of 1940. Even though *Graf Spee* had been lost in commerce raiding, Admiral Raeder still believed in the old theory of *guerre de course*, and on October 14, 1940, he had persuaded Hitler to let him send the *Admiral Scheer* to operate in the North Atlantic and then move south of the equator. So *Admiral Scheer* had made her breakthrough in the Denmark Strait on October 31 and had been at sea ever since, attacking ships and convoys. One of her memorable actions was against Convoy HX 84 on November 5, when she sank five ships, but was foiled from sinking more by the gallant auxiliary cruiser *Jervis Bay*, which sacrificed herself to save the rest of the convoy.

Admiral Scheer had been moving south and east, sinking ships as she found them, southeast of Bermuda, west of Bathurst, on the Freetown-South America route. On Christmas Day, when *Raider 16* lay in her snug harbor at Kerguelen, *Admiral Scheer* had met *Raider 10* (*Thor*) and three supply ships 600 miles north of Tristan da Cunha. They had exchanged supplies there, and the *Admiral Scheer* had come on northeast on the Cape Town-Freetown route. She had recently come into the Indian Ocean, on the Durban-Australia route, and was not finding it very successful, and was in need of diesel fuel, so Captain Krancke was pleased to learn of Rogge's capture of the tanker.

Berlin was nothing if not thorough. If Rogge was going to be handing out supplies in the middle of the Indian Ocean, he might as well supply everybody in sight—so seemed the theory. The supply ship *Tannenfels* was in the area, and needed fuel to get back to Bordeaux where she was headed. The Italian submarine *Perla* was in these waters and also needed supplies. So the confusion mounted. It ascended to a new height when Rogge learned that through a mixup, supplies scheduled for *Raider 16* had been loaded aboard the wrong ship and it would be a long time before he got them. But the confusion served one useful purpose; Berlin was not looking carefully at the problem of *Raider 16* and her shored-up bottom, and Rogge was to be permitted to continue operational instead of ordered home as a cripple.

Berlin was ever interfering. Rogge sent a message telling the Admiralty that the diesel oil he had aboard was 32.6APL. Berlin said the quality was not good enough for *Admiral Scheer*, so when the ships rendezvoused, *Raider 16* was to pump out her own tanks, give *Admiral Scheer* what she wanted, and then fill up from *Ketty Brovig* with the so-called "inferior" fuel.

The supply business began. On February 8, *Raider 16* met *Speybank* and took on hard stores from her, then dismissed her and sent her off to a new rendezvous.

On February 10, *Tannenfels* showed up, after having been lost for three days because her radio officer had deciphered a signal carelessly and she had gone to the wrong latitude. *Tannenfels* brought a bonus: Lieutenant Dehnel and the prize crew of *Durmitor*, who had been interned for a time by the Italians after delivering the prize ship. The Germans had suffered every conceivable indignity from the Italians, Dehnel said, and had finally escaped to the safety of the freighter *Tannenfels* when the British began advancing on Somaliland and the Italians grew frightened. Dehnel spent an evening telling Captain Rogge stories about the Italian war effort, and all Rogge could do was shake his head in wonder.

Next day the captain was shaking his head in worry, for he had a million things to do, it seemed, and no time in which to do them. First, *Speybank* had to be filled with diesel fuel from *Raider 16* and gotten ready to go on her own. Second, *Ketty Brovig*'s prize crew must be replaced by Lieutenant Dehnel and his men—the experienced ones. Third, the civilians from *Tannenfels* who had almost no experience must be distributed among the experienced crews, prisoners must be put into *Tannenfels*, and all three ships must share out provisions from among themselves and from *Raider 16.* Each ship must have adequate flags, sextants, chronometers, boats, charts, medicine, and a dozen other items that seem simple when handled by supply officers ashore, but which are not meant to be interchanged in detail on the high seas.

All this had to be done in two days.

Somehow it was done, and on February 13, the squadron got under way to meet *Admiral Scheer*.

Meet her they did, on the next day, and the lookouts had a few nasty minutes as they reported, "Warship on the port bow"—and instead of turning away at high speed to escape, the captain headed the flotilla directly for the ship. But it ended well, when the lookouts recognized the triple turret that was the mark of the pocket battleship. The crewmen of *Admiral Scheer* were as surprised as the men of *Atlantis*, for they had begun to believe they were moving to a convoy and, of course, that would mean an Allied convoy in these waters.

It was all straightened out in a matter of minutes after the masts came up on the horizon. Commodore Rogge paraded his flotilla for the warship, and then, in spite of roughening seas, he took the whaleboat and went aboard the *Admiral Scheer* to pay a courtesy call. The weather grew so rough, however, that it was apparent they were in the tail of a hurricane, and so the boat was called up, Rogge jumped in, and sped off—leaving a disconsolate Adjutant Mohr who had missed the leap and was left aboard the warship for at least a day.

The ships headed south to find peaceful waters where they could transfer fuel and foods. *Ketty Brovig* got lost, but showed up two days late, and *Admiral Scheer* took 1,200 tons of diesel oil from her tanks, fuel she found to be quite good enough. They remained at this rendezvous, 500 miles northeast of Mauritius, and the captains exchanged information and ideas, while the crews talked over their war experiences. They also traded curiosities: the raider giving every man on *Scheer* a fountain pen which came from one of their captures. *Admiral Scheer* responded with a gift of fresh eggs. She had recently captured the British refrigerator ship *Duquesa*. The raider took on 150,000 eggs, and for the next two weeks the men had all the eggs they wanted. For the first few days eggs went down fine, six or eight a day, because the men of the raider had not seen an egg for months. So they gobbled fried eggs, scrambled eggs, omelettes, boiled eggs, soufflés, and finally after two weeks there were still so many eggs that they had to be thrown overboard.

After two days, it was time to part, and the two captains agreed on their new hunting grounds: *Admiral Scheer* would search southwest of the Seychelles, taking those areas the raider had searched earlier. *Atlantis* (*Raider 16*) would move south and east of the Seychelles in new territory.

So *Raider 16* moved away from the rendezvous, *Tannenfels* was sent back to Bordeaux, and *Ketty Brovig* sent to the rendezvous off the Saya de Malha Bank. *Speybank* was to be used as an auxiliary or scout ship. Captain Rogge sent her out on his flank with orders to report by use of specially arranged message patterns if she saw anything. On February 20, Lieutenant

Breuers sighted a medium-sized tanker and kept contact with her out of sight of the raider. Later in the day Rogge took over and sent *Speybank* back to a rendezvous, and still later he discovered that the tanker was the French naval tanker *Lot*, accompanied by a pair of submarines and best left alone.

So he moved away.

On February 21, Rogge met *Speybank* and they went hunting again, and *Speybank* found a target. It turned out to be the *SS Africa Maru*, a Japanese freighter and not a useful target at all.

There was to be another rendezvous with *Scheer* just west of the 60th parallel, and Captain Rogge steered there, arriving on February 25. But instead of finding the *Admiral Scheer*, he discovered her prize, the British *Advocate*, a 7,000-ton tanker. Where was *Admiral Scheer*? She was on her way home. The reason was simply that this area of the ocean was beginning to swarm with British warships. The cruiser *Glasgow* had sighted *Admiral Scheer* (by use of an airplane) and tried to follow her. But Captain Krancke's sixth sense guided him and he decided to quit the Indian Ocean. He sped along on a straight course all day, shadowed by the British, then took evasive action on the night of February 22, and began moving away from the enemy. It was really a very narrow escape, with the British East Indies Station signaling *Glasgow* to follow and shadow but not to attack unless necessary, since four other British warships were being brought to bear on *Admiral Scheer*. But Captain Krancke was shrewd. He never came back to the rendezvous.

Captain Rogge did not understand what had happened, but he did understand that Captain Krancke had chosen his prize crew for *Advocate* hastily (which was quite true). The crew was so sloppy and so unruly that Rogge despaired of their ability to move the British *Advocate* to Bordeaux—but he sharpened her crew up as best he could and sent them off. (They arrived safely two months later.)

The raider spent the next three weeks uneventfully cruising in the area northeast of Mauritius. On March 21, *Speybank* came up, and Lieutenant Breuers was recalled to the raider, while the inexperienced young Lieutenant Schneidewind took over for him as prizemaster. Schneidewind made it home safely in May and his ship was converted to an auxiliary minelayer. Schneidewind took her out again on a military mission this time, and she served well until lost in the Pacific, much later. *Ketty Brovig*, which had been detailed to *Atlantis* for a time, was sent off by the German Admiralty to do service for other raiders, and was sighted by the aircraft of the British cruiser *Canberra* on March 2, in the company of another German ship, the *Coburg*. The latter was suspected of being a disguised raider and sunk by gunfire at long distance. Seeing the turn of events, the prize crew of *Ketty Brovig* scuttled her. So *Raider 16* lost her invaluable tanker.

Meanwhile, Berlin had come to some new conclusions. In Italy and her waters the battle was turning against the Axis powers, and the Italian submarines were desperately in need of fuel and supplies that they could not get for themselves. Cruising in the area, *Raider 16* was assigned the task of shepherding at least one of these submarines, the *Perla*.

A rendezvous point was established, but the submarine did not appear. Finally *Raider 16* located her by radio, and discovered that she was waiting 120 miles south of the correct position of rendezvous. (Berlin was not the only naval staff headquarters which made errors; Rome made them too, obviously.) *Perla* was a coastal submarine and she had not had a good war. Much of her time had been spent in harbor at Massawa under almost constant air attack from the British, and her crew was disillusioned and disconsolate. Neither crew nor captain had any taste at all for the war, and the captain confided to Rogge that every time he saw a masthead he dived and stayed under water until it went away. It was the best way he could think of to remain out of trouble.

The Italians needed everything, from cigarettes to charts, and Captain Rogge did what he could for them, contemptuous as he was of their fighting spirit. He gave them 70 tons of fuel, too. They were to fuel again from another German ship and then make their way back to European waters. *Perla* was to patrol off South Africa until April 8, but Rogge knew the captain would not do so.

In any event, *Perla* made her way home to Italy, and her captain was received by Il Duce himself and honored for his valiant service in the Red Sea and the Indian Ocean. So was Bernhard Rogge, as far as that was concerned. He was awarded the Medaglia di Bronzo al Valor Militar for reasons that would never be completely clear to anyone.

CHAPTER TWENTY-ONE

Taking the ZamZam

In a subtle and gradual way, Captain Rogge's war had changed drastically since he left Germany in the winter of 1940. The British had diverted much of their traffic from Australia and New Zealand around through the Panama Canal rather than send it into the Indian Ocean where so much had been sunk. The raiders had accomplished what the German Admiralty sent them out to do: ships now moved in convoy, tying up many war vessels; they moved slowly, tying up the British economic effort; mails had become unreliable and confidence in the war was decreased in the colonies; the need for extra personnel everywhere drained the trained manpower; large defense units had to be sent to the colonies. In other words, the German raiders, a handful of them, were hurting the British war effort sorely, and *Raider 16* was the most effective of the lot.

The war had changed in another way that was not so pleasant for Captain Rogge's delicate sense of honor. It was becoming more and more difficult to refrain from shooting first and asking questions later. Intercepted messages and just the volume of radio traffic itself told Rogge that the British buildup was becoming serious in the Indian Ocean, and it had already become an important matter in the Atlantic. As the war continued, the merchant captains learned better how to deal with raiders, and began paying attention to the British Admiralty rules where before they had delighted in breaking them.

A few months earlier, interrogating one of his captured merchant captains, Rogge inquired how the captain made his reports to the port captain when he arrived at Còlombo.

"I usually call on him at gin time," said the captain grinning

133

in delight at the question. That meant between 6 and 7 P.M. "He is in a hurry to get to his club and says, '*Must* you come at this time? You didn't sight anything, did you?' I always say 'No' and he is happy because otherwise we would both have to fill out endless questionnaires in fourteen copies."

But by the spring of 1941 the happy-go-lucky merchant skippers had seen enough of their brothers torpedoed and taken by submarines and raiders so that they took the war seriously. As noted, Rogge had been forced to change the tactics of *Raider 16.* Once he could close in on his victim in the daylight hours, raise his flags, and fire a warning shot across her bows. That was no longer true. Then he had tried trickery of various kinds, as with the *Ole Jacob* and the *Teddy,* but cunning worked only if he could get close enough. And that was the trouble these days. After the survivors of *Ole Jacob* landed in Japan, the British redoubled their warnings to merchant ships traveling alone: for safety's sake they must not let another ship approach them day or night, no matter what the cause or excuse.

The merchant ships were paying attention.

Consequently, Rogge's tactics evolved from gentility to brutality. First, he had tried to stop a ship by firing a round across its bow. That had worked once or twice. Then he had begun using one shot from one of the forward 150 mm. guns placed across the bows. That had worked once. Then had come a full salvo over the target, and that had worked, too, in its way. But the problem was that the British Admiralty *insisted* that merchantmen begin transmitting distress calls the minute they were fired upon, and the merchantmen began following orders, almost without exception. Thus a capture like that of *Speybank* was unusual in that there was no resistance, no attempt to warn shore stations and the ships at sea. For every *Speybank* there were two *Mandasors*, which would signal and signal until the radio was shot away, and even then would fight to the last to escape.

With this increase in resistance, Rogge felt he had no alternative but to open fire with all guns directly on the target and at the closest possible range, aiming to hit the radio cabin and the aerial to knock out transmissions first of all. Particularly since he had lost the second airplane, he was in no position to try trickery or cunning. Distressing as it might be personally, he accepted the new kind of war, and carried it out with grim efficiency.

Early in April *Raider 16* cruised east of Durban, heading

southeast, then northwest, then due south, sliding over to the east, to the west again, then back due south. On April 5 the lookouts spotted a vessel which lay to docilely and was not even fired upon—but she turned out to be the Vichy French *Chenonceux* carrying Senegalese troops to Madagascar. She was boarded and identified and let go on her way, for there was no reason to believe the Vichy men would inform the British of the German ships's position or identity.

Raider 16 now received orders to move out of the Indian Ocean and into the Atlantic, so she crossed around well south of her original track, rounded the Cape of Good Hope, and headed northwest toward mid-Atlantic. Rogge did not know it, but he was having even then a very narrow escape from the growing British defenses. Either the Frenchman reported him or some ship he did not see saw *Raider 16*, for on April 7 the British command in South Africa had word that a suspected German naval vessel was passing south of the Cape, and several airplanes were sent out on patrol in the next two or three days. Visibility was very poor in these waters during this autumn month and *Raider 16* was not spotted.

So a week passed, and *Raider 16* reached a point in mid-Atlantic 1,300 miles west of Lüderitz, and came into a square which had been set aside by the German Admiralty as a meeting place for several ships. *Atlantis* (*Raider 16*) was to secure stores from the supply ship *Alsterufer*. She was to pick up Navigator Kamenz from the supply ship *Nordmark*—Kamenz having completed his journey around the world and having delivered his important documents to Berlin. She was also to meet with *Raider 41* (*Kormoran*) so that Rogge might confer with Captain Detmers to their mutual advantage.

When *Raider 16* arrived at the rendezvous point, only the supply ship *Dresden* was there, and she had nothing for Rogge. At one point she was supposed to have taken on fresh foods for the raider, and she had done so; but pulling into Santos Brasil, she had been told by the naval attache at Rio that she was to turn over these supplies to the *Babitonga* for delivery to the raider. Captain Jaeger of the *Dresden* had pointed out that the other ship had no cold room and the supplies would spoil in the temperatures above 100°F., but a naval attache is a naval attache and this one brooked no interference with instructions. So the fresh provisions were transferred, and spoiled, and that was that.

Rogge was very angry, for he and his men had been at sea for more than a year. They needed fresh fruit, vegetables, and potatoes.

Vowing vengeance against that naval attache, Rogge took what *Dresden* could give him—potatoes and fresh water plus some other supplies, picked up two men traveling under the names of Meyer and Mueller, who were really Petty Officers Froehlich and Dittmann of the sunken *Graf Spee*, and went off a-raiding again, telling Captain Jaeger to stay where he was and await *Kormoran* and the others. Rogge then headed back east.

An hour after leaving *Dresden*, the raider sighted a large ship bearing southeast. It was a proper time, under the new conditions, for Captain Rogge to launch an attack, for it was just that darkness of night before dawn. The ship was blacked out, but she stood against the moon so clearly that Rogge could not only see her but thought he could recognize her for specifically what she was. Four years earlier, Bernhard Rogge had represented the German navy in the 6-meter international yacht races that were part of the coronation celebration of George VI. He raced here and there in England during the festivities and was invited by British officer acquaintances to visit the Royal Naval College at Dartmouth. There, in the broad anchorage, among the yachts and small workboats, he saw two merchant ships. They were old and odd—the oddest thing about them being that they sported four masts each. So Rogge had inquired.

They were Bibby Line steamers, said Rogge's naval acquaintances, old troop transports left over from World War I, which were used by the navy under charter for training cadets.

Rogge had noted the strange silhouettes, and forgotten them—but here in the darkness of the subtropical night in the South Atlantic, the memory was recalled. A Bibby liner. An English ship. Undoubtedly being used as a troop transport, said Rogge to himself.

And so he prepared to attack.

Here is Rogge's own story of the attack:

Her size and suspicious movements made me wonder whether she was in fact being used as an auxiliary cruiser, and as we followed cautiously in her wake, I made up my mind to get within range of her at daybreak and make a surprise attack. I wanted at all costs to prevent her from

sending an SOS, as the South Atlantic was narrower and
better patrolled than our previous operational area; our only
hope was to attack with every gun that would bear. My plans
had to be expedited when the ship began to transmit a signal—
quite a harmless one at first, "What station is that?" but we
could not know whether her next one would be QQQ or RRR.
The ship was now standing out clearly against the early
morning sky and we identified her definitely as one of the
Oxfordshire class, though we still could not see whether she
was armed nor could we distinguish the colors of her ensign.
I hesitated no longer and at 9,200 yards opened fire. . . .

What Captain Rogge did not know was to hurt him sorely.
The key was that the ship was, indeed, an old Bibby liner, but
she had become the pride of the Egyptian fleet, and Egypt was
at least nominally independent and neutral in this war. The ship,
now called the *ZamZam*, after the holy well in Mecca, carried
202 passengers, of whom 73 were women and 35 were children.
There were 138 Americans, 26 Canadians, 25 British, 5 South
Africans, 4 Belgians, an Italian, a Norwegian, and 2 Greek
nurses aboard. Or to break down the passenger list in another
way that would be unhappily significant to Rogge, there were
120 missionaries aboard.

Besides the passengers, the ship was captained by the
Scotsman William Gray Smith, and carried a crew of 128, most
of them Egyptians.

When the shooting began, most of the passengers were sound
asleep in their cabins. Charles J. V. Murphy, an editor of
Fortune magazine, was one of the passengers, and he later
described the affair in an article in *Life*:

A blind animal instinct drove me out of the cabin to the
deck, on the starboard side, opposite the sun, which had not
yet risen. From somewhere, quite near, came several loud
reports. The atmosphere tightened into a tense, spiralling
scream, and even as I shrivelled against the bones of my
body, the water directly abeam, less than 100 yards away,
rose up in two crackling columns and subsided. There was
another salvo, after which the ship shook and trembled, and
I heard a tearing, rending noise. In the dark—all the lights
were out—I crossed over to the port side, and the moment I

stepped out on deck I saw the German raider. She was broadside on, so close I could count her bridge decks, and if ever
a ship looked the role, she did—a ship of ambush, very low
in the water, black against the dawn. Even as I looked several
long red flashes spurted forward and abaft the funnel, and as
I raced back to the cabin the passageway behind me heaved
and filled with smoke. That shot, I think, hit the lounge. I
heard a child cry and a hoarse, hurt voice screaming . . .

The firing continued.

The bloody bastards are going to sink us without a trace,
thought Captain William Gray Smith, as he later told Murphy.

The first salvo had missed. The second salvo was on target
and one shell smashed the radio cabin. Captain Smith jerked the
engine telegraph to stop then, and ordered the ship turned
broadside to the raider to show that she had stopped.

Captain Smith went to the bridge—what was left of it—and
tried to send a Morse signal to the Germans, but the wires had
been cut away from his Morse blinker and it would not work.
He sent an Egyptian cadet to find him a flashlight. Meanwhile
the firing went on, 55 shells poured toward the ship at close
range and only 6 of them struck the *ZamZam*. It was the worst
shooting by *Raider 16* so far in the war. It ended only when
Captain Smith got his flashlight and was able to signal.

The crew got the boats over the side, but having gotten them
over, the crewmen jumped in and tried to leave with the half-
filled boats. Men, women, and children went quickly into the
water. One wounded man was helped into a boat and it left so
quickly that his wife fell into the sea.

Within half an hour all the boats were down and milling about
the *ZamZam*. Life rafts were in the water. The sea was full of
bobbing heads. Then the raider came around the other side of
the *ZamZam* and began the rescue. Lines were thrown to the
boats. The Egyptians tried to climb up, forgetting the passengers. The Germans shook them off. The lines were thrown again
and the Egyptians tried to climb again. The Germans were
getting ready to shoot the sailors off the ropes.

Then around came the two motor launches, commanded by
Adjutant Mohr and Leutnant Fehler. They rounded up the boats,
put them alongside the raider in neat pattern, and then went
aboard the *ZamZam*.

Smith lost no time in letting Mohr know the extent of the mistake the Germans had made, and the adjutant's heart fell when he learned of the number of missionaries and neutral Americans.

In his mind's eye, Mohr could see the headlines.

"A second *Lusitania!*"

"A new act of barbarism!"

Ship surrendered, the Germans did what they could to salvage the passengers' effects—particularly since most men and women had gone over the side in their night clothes. The boarding party dutifully went through bureaus and closets, finding ladies' underwear and men's trousers so the unwanted passengers of the raider might be decent if not exactly comfortable. It was a labor of love—for the *ZamZam* was heeling sharply as they worked and seemed likely to capsize at any moment. But that, too, passed. When she had taken 12 feet of water in the holds, she steadied and the Germans spent four hours stripping her of supplies, including those of the ship's bar.

As Mohr worked the *ZamZam*, Rogge directed the operations aboard the raider itself. Each boat was pulled up to the gangway, and the ablebodied climbed up. The wounded were taken up in the stretchers and the children in hemp baskets.

Aboard, passengers and crew were separated, the crew going aft and the passengers remaining on the main deck around the hatch. When the sun came up, the women and children were taken below.

"All the while," wrote Murphy, "the two motor boats shuttled back and forth carrying stuff to the raider from the *ZamZam* which was abeam, listing heavily to port and looking strangely tranquil. This was looting—extremely efficient looting. An endless chain of German sailors passed the hatch, shouldering boxes of provisions, cigarettes, radios, phonographs, suitcases, even a child's tricycle. . . .

"Nobody told us anything. We just sat and watched—bumming cigarettes from the farsighted ones who had crammed extra cigarettes into their pockets. That noon, volunteers brought food in metal bowls from the galley—a thick soup together with lime juice. . . ."

In the afternoon, several passengers including Murphy were selected by Adjutant Mohr for interview by Rogge.

They were taken to the topside and ushered into what Murphy

called a "beautiful little room with a handsome table, uphol-
stered settee, and hung with gay chintz curtains . . ."

Rogge stood up and shook hands with them all. He apolo-
gized for the sinking and then outlined his justification—the
ZamZam was running without lights in radio silence and
operating under British Admiralty direction.

So the 300 rescued from the *ZamZam* were taken care of, and
the Germans wished mightily they had never seen her at all, for
as Mohr recalled it, here was a typical moment of the day with
the passengers:

"Where can I get some milk? It's time for Susie to have her
milk."

"Can you tell me where the sick bay is? Perhaps I can find
some diapers there?"

"Have you got lifejackets for all of us?"

"Can someone fetch my glasses and my manicure case? I left
them in the ship. Cabin 237."

"Where shall we sleep tonight?"

"When do you think we can get off this ship?"

The answer to the last question, for which every German
officer thanked his stars, turned out to be in a matter of hours.
For Rogge had told *Dresden* to stay in the rendezvous zone, lest
perhaps *Raider 41* show up with prisoners to be transported to
a neutral port. Now Rogge had the prisoners, and he pushed
Raider 16 back to find *Dresden* and get rid of them. Meanwhile
he did everything possible to create a good impression among
the Americans, knowing full well the propaganda problem of
what he had done. Rogge found a solid gold chalice that
belonged to some of the missionaries and made sure it was
returned. The ladies and the men got as many of their posses-
sions as could be saved for them. They were treated graciously
and even generously, because Captain Rogge wanted no trouble
with America if he could avoid it.

Captain Rogge headed for the rendezvous with *Dresden*. Here
also was *Alsterufer*, loaded with fresh and preserved foods,
ammunition, and all other supplies that *Raider 16* needed badly,
plus three new airplanes and three new prize officers. One of the
prize officers was an old gentleman who liked to come into the
wardroom in bedroom slippers and shirtsleeves. Rogge had very
specific ideas about discipline on his ship. Officers and men were
always turned out smartly, shoes shined and in full uniform, unless

they happened to be playing such a role as that of Japanese house-wife, and even then they wore their kimono clean and with a flair. So the old gentleman was loaded aboard *Dresden* along with the *ZamZam* prisoners and dispatched back toward Europe. The second duty officer was also ill-assigned: he had been blown up in Norway and received such a severe concussion that he was fit for limited duty only, the provision being that he always keep his head protected from the hot sun. But the third officer was perfectly fine, and so Rogge thanked the personnel bureau for striking one in three, and retained his genial dislike for navy bureaucrats.

Dresden was dispatched. Rogge argued with Berlin that to prevent international incidents the best thing possible would be to send her to the Canary Islands or some other neutral spot nearby, but Berlin insisted that *Dresden* come into European waters where she would be useful to the high command. So she sailed for St. Jean de Luz on the west coast of France, arriving there safely.

On her arrival the story of the sinking came out in the Allied and neutral press. They called the raider *Tamesis* in most of the articles, including the special report written for *Life* in June by Correspondent Murphy. Soon the raider concept was taken up vigorously by the newspapers in the United States, and even in Murphy's article Captain Rogge could not emerge unscathed, for Murphy referred to the affair from the point of view of passengers as "brutal, wholly unnecessary shelling of an unarmed ship—a ship not only stopped but hopelessly stricken. . . ." And the Egyptian officers of the ship complained that the *ZamZam* was a neutral ship under international law. Captain Rogge had summarized his conditions of warfare in the ship's log, and stated his own position toward his raiding activities:

In all circumstances I have tried to make war in accordance with the old raider tradition of "fairness," by which I mean that where possible I never fired for longer than was absolutely necessary to break down the enemy's resistance and destroy his radio. Where we had a chance of identifying the ship as a tanker or a particularly valuable prize and could take a chance on her sending a distress signal, we refrained from opening fire. We have treated our prisoners and survivors as we would wish to be treated ourselves in similar circum-stances; we have tried to make their lot as easy as possible.

But it was no good. Rogge had promised the Americans that they would be transferred to a neutral ship or landed at a neutral port. Berlin overruled Rogge and sent *Dresden* to France. So Captain Rogge, who tried harder than any other German naval officer to retain whatever gentility remained in warfare, was tagged as one of the "butchers."

CHAPTER TWENTY-TWO

The New Record

For a week *Raider 16* lay in the rendezvous area 500 miles north of Tristan da Cunha, taking supplies from *Alsterufer* and *Nordmark*. Then on April 27 with heavy holds and light hearts, the Germans parted from the supply ships and headed for the Cape Town-Freetown route, having word from Berlin that this area was at the moment very weakly guarded by British defense forces. The men loafed and read the mail—the first mail they had received in more than a year. Some work was done to transform the ship—she could no longer masquerade as *Tamesis* after the exposure to the Americans—and her upper works were painted grayish and the name *Brastagi* adorned her stern. She was supposed to be a Dutch motorship. To be completely believable, her hull color should have been changed from dark to light gray, but a heavy swell arose during the hull painting and Captain Rogge delayed the work for the time being.

The life of a raider was a matter of constant surprise and innovation. Berlin had sent out three new aircraft, of the Arado 196 design. They had not, however, sent out any technicians from the factory or any written instructions on assembling the craft. So Flying Officer Bulla, Stabsfeldwebel Borchert, and his mechanics had their hands full for two weeks until they put one of the machines together and Borchert flew it successfully. He came back singing the praises of the new plane: it was smaller, faster, and took off in a shorter distance. It handled better as an airplane and was handled more easily by the crew in getting it over the side and into the water. On May 1, Borchert, the pilot and Bulla, the observer went off to investigate a smoke cloud, but the ship *City of Exeter* was such a fast one that *Raider 16* did not ever catch up with her.

On May 4, the raider met the merchantman *Babitonga*, which had been sent out of the Brazilian port of Santos to act as auxiliary for the warship. After a brief meeting, Captain Rogge sent *Babitonga* off to wait at 30° South, 15° West, disguised as the Dutch SS *Jaspara*. Nine days later, on the night of May 13–14, *Raider 16* had reached the Cape Town-Freetown route and was cruising when her lookouts reported a ship. Captain Rogge thought she might be a Dane, and decided to try to capture her with the signal lamp. But she went right on, ignoring the signal. Rogge ordered them to shine the searchlight on her bridge, but this, too, was ignored. Then he lost patience and began shooting; a round was fired across her bows and she set off then on a new course, to escape. Captain Rogge ordered Gunnery Officer Kasch to fire for effect, and to knock out the radio cabin first. The first salvo set the ship on fire and men began to abandon her. In half an hour she sank; *Raider 16* picked up survivors and steamed away, Rogge learning in his questioning of the survivors that the ship was the British SS *Rabaul* bound from England for Cape Town with coal and other cargo. Her watch officer was an old salt of sixty-four called back to wartime duty, and he had seen the signals of *Raider 16* but had simply moved to the other side of the bridge, on the basis that thus he could ignore them and the raider would go away. Seven men were killed and nine wounded that night.

Captain Rogge was now considering a much longer stay at sea than anyone had envisaged. Originally, Berlin had hoped that the raiders not sunk might stay out as long as a year. Rogge had passed a year in March and was now thinking in terms of a year and a half, knowing he had provisions for two years, perhaps, but knowing also that his crew could not manage so long a journey. But if he were to stay out, he must be careful, so now he stopped the motors and began to drift in the Cape Town-Freetown sea-lane. On the night of May 17 they were drifting in the calm sea and bright moonlight, a night that would have been perfect had there been no war. Rogge was on the bridge deck, half asleep, just after midnight when the coxswain and a signalman together announced the appearance of two blots on the horizon. Soon Rogge could tell that they were two large ships steaming in line, and heading directly toward the raider.

He sounded the alarm.

On came the ships, and it was not very long before Captain Rogge could tell that they were warships, and large ones. They moved ahead at 14 knots, standing between *Raider 16* and the moon, which meant they were silhouetted but that the raider was not, for the moon shone straight on the raider and cast no shadow, and she was so lucky that behind her were massed clouds that blackened the horizon. The danger was that *Raider 16* might show sparks if they started the cold motors too quickly or tried to run them too fast, and Rogge was clearly aware of that danger because it had happened to him before. Slowly, ever so slowly, the motors were started and he began to steer to starboard of the big ships.

It was perhaps half an hour later that he turned stern on, to give the least possible silhouette, and at about this time recognized the ships: one as a Nelson class battleship (33,900 tons) and the other as an aircraft carrier (probably 23,000 tons), each with a speed exceeding 30 knots, the battleship carrying nine 16-inch guns plus a dozen 6-inch guns, and the carrier mounting 70 planes. Obviously this was more than the "token" force mentioned by Berlin, and just as obviously Rogge would be very lucky to get away from them.

As he was hoping and waiting, up came a whistle from the engine room—a whistle and then a croaking voice:

"What's happening up on the bridge? There seem to be two ships out there. Aren't you going to attack them?"

The officer of the watch spoke gently down the tube, identifying the ships. From the engine room came a deep, thoughtful silence.

The British ships came up quickly and quietly, and Captain Rogge was certain they had seen him, but they altered course and passed astern of the raider paying no attention at all to her. The range was perhaps 7,000 yards, so close that from the bridge of the German ship the officers could see the bow wave of the battleship. It seemed hours before the British ships disappeared over the horizon, and the men of the raider could feel safe.

It was *just* an hour later that something happened in the combustion system—a shower of flame and sparks shot up the funnel and sprayed the ship and the water around it. Had the British warships been in sight, *Raider 16* would have looked like a Fourth of July display to them, and it would undoubtedly have been the end of her. Both engines were stopped and the ship lay helplessly in the sea while the trouble was repaired. All this while Rogge and his men looked over at the horizon where the British giants had disappeared, fearing they might see something and come back. But all was serene to the north. The British ships were on their way from Walvis Bay to the North Atlantic, and they were not looking back. Now came many ships. There was a Vichy French convoy, which they hailed in gay French. There was a Greek, *Master Elias Kulukundis*, traveling under charter by the Swiss government, and thus very much a neutral. There was an American, unneutral, named the *Charles H. Cramp*, which could not be disturbed.

It was not until May 24 that the men of the raider saw action again. On that day Bulla went out in the seaplane to scout, and came back waggling the wings of the plane, which alerted Captain Rogge to battle stations because it meant he had sighted something that ought to be of interest to the raider. It was a 4,500-ton merchant ship, just over the horizon. Learning her course and speed from Bulla, Captain Rogge could lie back and move just fast enough to keep her in range, waiting for night to come in and then attack. That is what he did, moving in under cover of darkness to begin shelling the other ship. Rogge was not taking the same care these days that he had before.

His own situation was edgier, as he could see that night in the passing of the two great monsters of the sea in the moonlight. He did not dare take chances on being "DF'd"— tracked down by the very good British radio direction finder system that could operate from his radio emanations. Berlin scoffed, but Rogge had experience: in fact when Lieutenant Breuers was operating the *Speybank* as a scout for *Raider 16* back in February, Breuers discovered that he could DF *Raider 16* himself from the merchant ship, and he proved it by maintaining contact with the ship just through listening to her transmissions. Breuers had done the same with the French naval tanker *Lot*.

So this attack on the 4,500-ton merchantman was made swiftly and slashingly; the first salvo struck home, soon the funnel was blown off and the foremast broke in two and fires broke out in the deck cargo, which consisted largely of crated airplanes. The fires rose so high and seemed so dangerously near attracting attention that Rogge ordered the ship torpedoed. He did not often use torpedoes because *Raider 16* never seemed to have much luck with them. This night was no exception. The first torpedo missed, circled completely around the target, and came back to threaten *Raider 16* so definitely that Rogge had to dodge it. The second torpedo missed. The third struck home, and the ship went down in nine minutes. *Raider 16* sent out her boats and picked up the crew, except for 12 men who had been killed in the firing or had drowned in the water.

It was not a very pleasant night. It was not a very pleasant feeling—this realization that so far the men of *Raider 16* had caused the death of some 60 men of the sea. That was not to say that the Germans were squeamish about their calling—they were warriors of the sea and they were ready to deal death or to take death as it came. Yet there *was* a difference between a raider and an ordinary warship. The submarine commander did not come face to face with his victims. The bomber pilot did not have to operate on the man whose leg had just been blown off by a shell from the pilot's gun. The cruiser captain did not have to see the stricken looks on the faces of men in the water.

The men of *Raider 16* were growing tired, and there was no doubt about it. Captain Rogge did not like his war, he did not like his Führer, he did not like the manner in which the high command was propagandizing. These days the navy, and the raider in particular, was being used more and more for propaganda purposes. Adjutant Mohr listened to the BBC and the American broadcasts when he wanted the truth about world war affairs. Take the matter of the *Ark Royal*, for example. The Germans were claiming to have sunk that carrier, but privately the German Admiralty was keeping the naval forces at sea up to date on the movements of the ship.

Rogge and his men were loyal Germans, and they were fighting the best and most effective war they knew how to fight for their Fatherland, but they were finding much that they did not like in the news from home.

Just after sinking this 4,500-ton freighter, the *Trafalgar*, Captain Rogge received confirmation of his fears about being DF'd from no less authority than Berlin—previously disbelieving Berlin. On May 5, three British auxiliary cruisers had begun moving in on another raider after notification of a bearing that was based on three short distress calls of no more than fifteen letters each. Also, he learned of the sinking of *Raider 33* (*Pinguin*) by HMS *Cornwall* on May 8, and the elimination of *Ketty Brovig* and the supply ship *Coburg*. Other raiders were moved rapidly around the chessboard of the ocean, but they were all finding the going difficult: many enemy cruisers and auxiliaries were out searching for them, and they found few merchant ships to prey upon. *Raider 41* (*Kormoran*) headed out for the waters beyond Ceylon and Sumatra. *Raider 45* (*Komet*) was searching the area west of Australia with very little luck. *Raider 37* (*Orion*) was spotted by a Sunderland flying boat in the Coral Sea and had a very narrow escape from sinking by a hurricane. Berlin was being very cautious and keeping the raiders *off the sea-lanes*, which meant they had very little chance of sinking anything, and even that evasion was not much good. *Raider 37* made her way into the Indian Ocean and promptly sighted two different British cruisers, against which she took successful evasive action. But evasive action was not the same as sinking ships.

The men of *Raider 16* (*Atlantis*) learned of the sinking of the battleship *Hood* and cheered, but with little qualms in their hearts because they knew how the British valued *Hood*, and how much stronger the British naval determination would become because of the sinking.

They learned of the bombing of the *Prinz Eugen* at Brest, and of the sinking of the *Bismarck* at the end of May. Three days after that sinking, *Raider 16* was back in the area of 12° West, 30° South, to meet *Babitonga* again, hand over the prisoners she had captured, and make plans for the future. Captain Rogge's engineers overhauled the engines of the raider while *Babitonga* went to transfer the prisoners to another supply ship and then return to accompany *Raider 16*.

The overhaul took nearly two weeks. It was June 11 when the engineering department had finished its work and could report that *Raider 16* was ready again for a long voyage. Berlin now ordered Captain Rogge onto the South American route and the north part of the Cape Town-Freetown route. On June 16, Captain Rogge and the men of the *Raider 16* completed 445 days constantly at sea, to break the record set by the raider *Wolf* in World War I and become the raider crew who had spent more time at sea than any other in history.

CHAPTER TWENTY-THREE

The Sea Change

With the sensitivity of a man who knew his environment and the war he was fighting, Captain Rogge could see that matters were changing for him every day, and not for the better.

The merchant raiders had proved to be a very serious thorn in the sides of the British Admiralty. During the last six months of 1940, merchant raiders sank 48 ships totaling 326,013 tons. During the first six months of 1941, merchant raiders sank 38 ships totaling 190,623 tons.

The first six months of 1941 were not nearly so successful for the raiders as the first period, but they were hurtful enough to Britain to make it necessary for her to take ever stronger action to put an end to the armed merchant raiders.

Besides *Raider 16* there were still three other raiders in action by the first of June, *Raider 36*, *Raider 41*, and *Raider 45*, but they were having considerable difficulty in keeping themselves supplied. *Raider 36*, for example, had steam turbine engines driven by oil, and these used about 800 tons of oil per month, as compared to the 200 tons used by *Raider 16* with her diesel motors. And targets were ever harder to find.

The reason for the "shortage" of merchant ships on the high seas was the increasing use of convoys by the British, and the raiders were in no position to interfere with convoy shipping. Further, the British Admiralty was in control of all shipping for herself and her Allies, and more and more Allied auxiliary cruisers, warships, and patrol planes were used on an ever more professional and effective basis. By the beginning of June the British Admiralty was certain that the Germans had many supply ships at sea, and within a few weeks nine of these ships were

149

taken, including *Raider 16*'s *Babitonga*, which was scuttled on June 21 at 2° 05′ North, 27° 42′ West.

Raider 16 was feeling the pinch, too. On June 17 she came upon the British ship *Tottenham* at night, in one of her now-usual attacks. *Tottenham* signaled for help, and was shelled unmercifully and sunk because she also returned fire against the raider. In the darkness 29 British sailors were rescued, 5 were killed, and 17 made their way out in a boat of their own, only to be lost at sea, the boat to drift into the harbor at Rio de Janeiro nine weeks later.

It gave Captain Rogge no pleasure to fire on ships that he knew were unequal to him, to kill men because they fought back. Yet he was a good officer to his navy, and he still would do what he was ordered to do in the service of his country as long as he could do it, distasteful to him as it might be. The logs of the raider show the facts, but Rogge's attitude toward his work is shown better in the book he produced after the war. He had very little to say about the sinking of *Tottenham* and the abandonment of that boat he could not find. It was not a matter which pleased or satisfied him.

On June 22, north of Brazil's Trinidad Island, *Raider 16* launched a night attack on the 5,000-ton British freighter *Balzac*. The freighter bravely began to use her radio but the Germans jammed the signal. She tried to zigzag and run, and the Germans began firing salvos. At the fortieth salvo the overheated forward guns and No. 5 gun refused to fire. Soon Kasch had to reduce his firing to one or two rounds at a time, and then Rogge was about to break off the action when *Balzac* surrendered. She had taken four hits from 190 rounds fired. Not very good shooting. Even more disturbing was the failure of the guns, for it gave indications that *Raider 16* was suffering from having been too long at sea.

Five days later, Captain Rogge was ordered to meet north of Tristan da Cunha with *Raider 37* (*Orion*) and supply her with enough fuel to last until September. Berlin informed him that it contemplated his return during the autumn and that he would be refueled before that time. Captain Rogge and Captain Weyher of *Raider 37* met, and Weyher demanded much more than the 700 tons of fuel allocated to him, but that is all he got; Rogge could be very stubborn. They parted companionably enough on July 6, and *Raider 37* moved west.

Berlin had ordered *Raider 16* to stay in the South Atlantic, raid at will, wait for resupply in the late summer, and then make a dash for home during the worsening weather of autumn. Rogge had other ideas. The North Atlantic seemed to be teeming with British cruisers, and some were working their way south. The South Atlantic was a very narrow strip of ocean to Rogge's mind, and he felt that the number of prisoners and ships captured in recent weeks had completely compromised his safety in that sea. Gunnery Officer Kasch assured him that the guns were still in good enough condition to fight. He had aboard 60 percent of his maximum of ammunition and plenty of fuel, with promise of resupply. His food and general supply situation was better than it had been a few months before. The main problem was the morale of the men, but he simply told them it was their duty to keep going, and they accepted his discipline. The idea would be to keep fighting, keep changing oceans until winter, and then make the breakthrough at the time when he had the best chance of success, the cold stormy months of midwinter.

Raider 16 then headed for the Pacific, estimating that the best hunting grounds left would be found around Australia, and also that their best chance of avoiding detection was in those waters. On July 9 they passed Gough Island, heading east, and then began the deep swing to travel well into the roaring forties, a good 12 degrees south of the Cape of Good Hope. Few British cruisers would expect a raider to be so far south of any normal shipping lanes.

They headed eastward, north of Prince Edward Island and south of St. Paul. They bucked gales and the usual heavy weather of the forties. They kept trying to send messages home, but Berlin did not receive them. Radio South Africa apparently did, because soon Radio Officer Wenzel caught a British signal reporting a German raider in the Kerguelen area. Once again Rogge was warned about the dangers of radio direction finding.

Raider 16 celebrated her 500th day at sea off the Crozet Islands, east of New Zealand. It was a dreary time, not an exciting one. The passage across the lower portion of the world had been stormy and uncomfortable, and at one point they had been forced to heave to for several days to ride out a gale. Here was September, and they had not met an enemy vessel since June 22. It was seven weeks since they had parted company with *Raider 37*, and they had seen nothing but sky and sea and one another in all that time So boring was life that even the advent of an albatross which was lured on deck brought a flurry of excitement.

Then, two hours after sunset on September 10, *Raider 16* made a contact, east of the Kermadec Islands. She was a poorly blacked-out merchant ship, headed east. Captain Rogge was sick of shooting first and asking questions afterward, and he decided to try to take her without firing. As *Raider 16* came up, the other ship began her distress call, "QQQQ . . ." warning other ships and shore stations that she was approached by a strange ship. The calls rang out loud and clear. Once again human failure attacked *Raider 16*: the radio men tried to jam, but forgot to plug in the jamming equipment, so it was some minutes before the calls of the other ship were drowned out. She identified herself in that time as *Silvaplana* and gave the world her position. Then *Raider 16* was on her, Rogge signaled by light that she was to stop at once, and cease using her radio. *Silvaplana* complied. The flaps were dropped on the guns and not a shot was fired, much to the raider captain's satisfaction.

Silvaplana was carrying a cargo of Balinese idols, coffee, wax, vanilla, teak, sago, tin, and rubber. Since she was unhurt and seaworthy, Captain Rogge decided to keep her on hand until he could supply her with fuel to send her to France. But there were problems.

Worst of these was the fact that the SOS had been broadcast so many times in the clear. Rogge hoped it had not been heard, but that hope was soon dashed when radio Raratonga and other stations began repeating the message. *Raider 16*'s operators quickly sent cancellations of the appeal, but these cancellations apparently did not impress British naval headquarters, for soon came a request that *Silvaplana* repeat the message in code, and since the ship's captain had destroyed his code books, the Germans could not do so. So they were already suspect, and they knew it. Captain Rogge had made a wide detour around New Zealand and turned several times before setting course for the Kermadecs to dodge the East Indies-North Australia naval screen that Berlin now knew about. Rogge sent *Silvaplana* 400 miles south of Tubusi Island to rendezvous and then went hunting again, but found nothing in the next few days and met *Silvaplana* to take 400 tons of her rubber as ballast for the raider. Then the prize was sent away again, for *Raider 16* was going to meet *Raider 45* (*Komet*) and the supply ship *Münster-land*.

As they approached the rendezvous, Rogge was reminded that the commander of *Raider 45* was Konteradmiral Eyssen. When the ships approached, and the captain of *Raider 45* indicated that he would come aboard *Raider 16*, he was given an admiral's salute by the raider's guns, and then piped aboard with all the ceremony he might have enjoyed if he were visiting the deck of a battleship in the North Sea.

Then came the difficult part. Rear Admiral Eyssen wanted some of the supplies from *Münsterland*, and it was never easy for a mere captain to refuse an admiral what he wanted. *Raider 45*, said the admiral, had been given stores only once, and those very inadequate. Rogge thought fast. He knew that his men were in worse shape than the admiral's, but how to prove it?

Calling in his surgeons, he worked out the proper figures for vitamins and essential foods for his ship, and those for *Raider 45*. He was able to show that *Raider 16* had received *no* fresh vegetables in 540 days, while *Raider 45* had been restocked five different times. He took the matter of potatoes, a basic German food. Once Rogge's original supply of potatoes had been exhausted, his men had received potato meals 35 times, the last four months earlier. *Raider 45* had potatoes regularly, the last time three days earlier.

Konteradmiral Eyssen was a fair man, and Captain Rogge's arguments were very convincing, so *Raider 45* contented herself with nothing more than a portion of *Raider 16*'s beer supply from the stores of *Münsterland*.

The transfer of supplies meant that *Raider 16*'s holds were full again, and theoretically she was ready for another year at sea. But she had been at sea for eighteen months without cessation, and after discussions with Konteradmiral Eyssen and the captain of *Münsterland*, Captain Rogge made up his mind definitely that they would head for home at the end of 1941. They would operate in the Pacific until October 19, then move to the South Atlantic, stop for a ten-day overhaul of the engines, operate for ten days, and then move north for the breakthrough, hoping to come in on the new moon of December 20, bringing the men home for Christmas. One could not say that Captain Rogge was discouraged, but he had noted the changes in his ship, his men, and the war situation with grave sensitivity. The

Americans had established their "neutrality zone" around the American continents, and the patrolling there was strong and frequent. The convoys were taking most ships between the major ports, and the frequency of radio messages showed how strong British sea power was becoming in all the far-flung waters which had been so easy to work for victims even six months earlier. When Rogge had come out, eighteen months earlier, he was alone and the first of the merchant raiders. Now the raiders had a reputation, the newspapers of the world were filled with exploits they had committed and many that they had not, and every Allied ship in the sea was alert for them. It had been quite a sea change.

CHAPTER TWENTY-FOUR

The Long Wait

The little flotilla sat quietly at the rendezvous, *Raider 16* filling her holds from those of *Münsterland*, while *Raider 45* made her preparations to head for home, accompanied by her last prize, the Dutch ship *Kota Nopan*, which she had captured on August 17 and kept with her. On September 24 the last goodbyes were said, Captain Rogge left the deck of the other raider and moved into his boat, fraternal waves were exchanged, and the admiral set off for his long voyage, the men of *Raider 16* looking enviously after the ship that was going home.

The radio operators of *Raider 16* organized record concerts, and the officers redoubled their efforts to interest the men in lectures on every imaginable subject, from Australian politics to personal experiences in Siberia, anything to keep the men busy and happy in this difficult time.

The indefatigable Adjutant Mohr had discovered a valuable chart when he searched the captain's cabin aboard the *Silvaplana*. It was the chart of *Silvaplana*'s own most recent voyage through the Pacific, and Rogge reasoned that this route must represent the British Admiralty's recommended course for ships traveling alone. He decided to steam along this lane, and made preparations to leave. On September 27, *Raider 16* called up the prize crew of *Silvaplana* and ordered them to take the ship to Bordeaux. Next day *Münsterland* sailed for Japan, where she would reload supplies and wait for the next opportunity to supply a raider. When that would be was not quite sure, for the British net was closing. It was harder than ever for any ships to run the gauntlet of British defense and make the breakthrough, and those raiders still at sea were growing tired.

First Lieutenant Kühn reported the *Atlantis* ready for action, and Captain Rogge, too, steamed away from this lonely spot of sea heading for the track of the *Silvaplana*. For nearly two weeks the raider searched this route, but with absolutely no success. The sun came up hot every morning, and sank redly into the sea every night. They encountered a squall or two, they saw flying fish and sometimes a manta ray; when they were near the islands the land birds circled them, and when they were far at sea the seabirds followed their ship, but of smoke or a mast there was never a trace. For a few days Borchert and Bulla went up every morning to see what they could find, but as they returned after an hour or so of flight, there was never a waggle of the wings—they found nothing. Then the weather turned sloppy, and it became very hard to use the plane. Captain Rogge considered the problem, and its solutions.

They were lying south of the Tuamotu archipelago. If the weather continued thus they might well lose the airplane in launching or recovering it. Besides, the men could use a little relaxation, and every one of them had dreams of tropical paradise. Rogge called Adjutant Mohr to his cabin and announced his decision.

"We are going to establish a new base for a series of operations," he said. He wanted Mohr to consider the Tuamotus.

After some discussion, they settled on the island of Vana Vana because it was one of the least inhabited of the Tuamotus, and had never been settled by a large group of foreign missionaries. Thus it was unlikely that Vana Vana would be "afflicted" with a radio. So the course was set, the announcement was made to the crew, and in high spirits the men of *Raider 16* set out for South Seas adventure.

Bulla scouted first in his airplane, flying over the broad lagoon where they would anchor, above the white sand and the green beyond. He and his pilot saw a village of reed huts with a Christian church whose steeple was made of palm leaves. Then, the reconnaissance finished, they reported back to the ship.

Captain Rogge brought *Raider 16* in, slowly and carefully, to a point near the shore. The shore fell away steeply so that at 50 yards off the beach he could stop with plenty of water beneath his keel. They stopped *Raider 16*, and Captain Rogge called Bulla to him. While the men played, Bulla would work— he was to fly three missions a day in search of enemy shipping.

Raider 16 would go on war watch, half the crew ready for action, the other half relaxed, and, if possible, every man would be given a chance to go ashore for a few hours—the first chance in the ten months since they left Kerguelen.

So the men did scramble ashore through the opening in the reef, in boats and rubber rafts, wearing pith helmets and white uniforms with shorts, for Captain Rogge insisted that his men appear in proper uniform no matter where they were, as a matter of morale and the honor of the German navy.

The natives of Vana Vana were friendly and welcomed them. The men ate native food and picked fresh coconuts, which they brought back by the scores. The ship traded flour for 500 coconuts as well.

After forty-eight hours, which meant six search trips for the airplane and shore leave for nearly every man of the crew, *Raider 16* moved on to Pitcairn Island, still flying off the plane regularly, but without success. A hundred miles northeast of Pitcairn, Rogge found a sheltered harbor at Henderson Island and the crew was landed again on this deserted volcanic island where not even insects seemed to live.

Pickings were so slim in the Pacific that Captain Rogge decided to speed up his trip a bit and move into the Atlantic sooner than he had expected. The moment the news came to the scuttlebutt that the ship was going to round the Horn, morale soared, for the crew were aching to get home and South Atlantic meant homeward to them. So they began the long trip, near the Falkland Islands, keeping just above the South Shetlands, and traveling through the cold foggy water of the Antarctic regions.

While rounding the Horn on October 29, Captain Rogge intercepted a German Admiralty message which spoke of the loss of the supply ship that was serving the submarines off Cape Town, and he promptly offered the services of *Raider 16* as supply vessel. The offer was as promptly accepted by Berlin, before they had left the snow squalls and unusually calm sea of the Cape. The first U-boat they would service would be *U-68* and the rendezvous was established at a point northeast of the one at which they had met *Dresden* and *Nordmark* six months before.

Two weeks later—November 13—*Raider 16* met the U-boat, and moved off to a position far from any sea-lanes. Captain Rogge was very nervous, for he had heard of meetings between

U-boats being interrupted by Allied warships. He was very careful not to use his radio, and to lead *U-68* away from the place stipulated by Berlin in its transmissions. Rogge was not at all sure that the German naval code was 100 percent safe, and much less certain about the security of his own position in any case.

It was fitting that Rogge should be worrying so on November 13, for this was the very day when Grand Admiral Raeder was meeting with Hitler to discuss the auxiliary cruisers and the future. When the *Bismarck* was sunk, Hitler was plunged into one of his frenzies against the navy. He had summoned Grand Admiral Erich Raeder to his hideaway in Bavaria and demanded an account of what had happened. That time Raeder was able to convince his commander that the loss of the *Bismarck* was unavoidable. But now, in the autumn of 1941, Hitler was again showing his basic distrust of surface ships in time of war, and he called for an explanation of the sudden drop in sinkings by the raiders.

Grand Admiral Raeder explained that the enemy was responding with the convoy system, which did not lend itself to attack by raiders, but rather to attack by submarines. Yet Raeder believed in auxiliary cruisers, and at that meeting he won Hitler's approval of a plan to send four more raiders out in 1942. He also wanted to send *Admiral Scheer* back to the Indian Ocean, but Hitler said No, for he was afraid that the pocket battleship might be lost there, and the propaganda defeat would be worse than anything she might win for Germany in physical victories.

Raeder subsided. But perhaps Der Führer would reconsider when *Raider 16* and *Raider 41* returned within a matter of weeks, so successful had they been.

Perhaps.

As Hitler and Raeder talked, Captain Rogge was meeting *U-68*, 530 miles southwest of St. Helena. The weather was so rough that they moved another 80 miles north. The commander of *U-68* was an old friend of Rogge's, Korvettenkapitän Merten, with whom he had sailed in small boats for the honor of Germany in quieter years. Merten came aboard *Raider 16* and the pair settled down in the wardroom for a drink and a talk. Rogge was disconsolate: Berlin had taken him at his word, and instead of asking that he help by refueling *one* U-boat, they seemed bent on making a supply ship of *Atlantis*, and also of keeping her almost in the middle of the busy Cape Town-Freetown sea-lane which had once been a hunting ground but was now alive with British hunters.

"After refueling your boat," he told Merten ruefully, "I had intended to overhaul my engines and then go on patrol for a few days. But now I have been ordered to refuel *U-126*."

"I know," said Merten. "That's Bauer's boat [Kapitänleutnant Bauer]. I read the signal."

"That may be very desirable in the interests of the war, you know," Rogge continued, "but it is very inconvenient for me and in any case I don't see the need for it. The supply ship *Python* is shortly due to cross the equator on her way to her area of St. Helena. Bauer could have refueled just as well from her."

Next day, the resupply of *U-68* was carried out in a heavy swell. She took oil and water, food and soap, cigarettes and clothing from the raider. There were more good times in the *Atlantis*'s wardroom, and then, on November 16, *U-68* slid away to operate off Angola and the mouth of the Congo River. *Raider 16* prepared to leave for what the German Admiralty referred to in its secret charts as "Flower Point Lily 10," at about 5° South, 22° West, almost due north of the spot where she had sunk *Tottenham* on June 17, and far too close to the sea-lane. The preparations consisted of some "hurry-up" work on the main engines.

Raider 16 was to have several more days of hunting before she had to meet the submarine, and Captain Rogge set out to the west, looking for enemy vessels. Flying Officer Bulla was the key to his search these days. On the second day he found a ship for them, but it turned out to be a neutral. On the third day he found another ship, but she was a fast vessel, and *Raider 16* could not catch her. On this day, the weather roughed up between takeoff and landing—one of the perennial threats to a raider's spotter plane—and on landing the seaplane damaged her supercharger. There were plenty of spare parts, including engines, but this damage meant engine replacement and that, in turn, meant twenty-four hours in which the seaplane would be out of service. And when she was back in service, the trade winds blew so hard that poor Bulla could not even take off. Finally, on November 21, Bulla managed to get the seaplane into the air and then on landing she capsized in the heavy swell, and it was an effort for *Raider 16*'s men to save crew and airplane both. They did save all, but the plane was so badly damaged this time that there was no hope of it getting into the air again that day, or the next day when the raider was scheduled to meet the submarine. Rogge was disappointed, partly because he wanted to search for more merchantmen, and partly because he thought it would be an excellent idea to have an air screen above when he met the submarine in these dangerous waters. Now he would have to do without air eyes, because the other two airplanes were still stowed in cases in the hangar deck.

So Navigator Kamenz put down his protractors and did a bit of figuring, and in the early hours of November 22, *Raider 16* arrived at the position known to the German Admiralty as Lily 10, which was located 350 miles northwest of Ascension Island.

There she waited.

CHAPTER TWENTY-FIVE

The Intruder

In the autumn of 1941 the British Admiralty noted a movement of U-boat activity toward the South Atlantic, and the British responded by moving more capital ships into the area to assist in the war against submarines and raiders. In November, the East Indies Station warned that the Admiralty believed U-boats could be expected to operate in the Cape area in the near future, as well as along the Atlantic coast of Africa.

Such operation was precisely what *U-68* was about to undertake to the north, and the U-boat Captain Rogge was to meet—*U-126*—was to do further south.

Sensing this increase in activity the British navy men grew restless and watchful, and kept on the lookout for enemy vessels.

The task had been assigned by Admiral Algernon Willis, shore commander of the South Atlantic, to a group headed by Captain A. W. S. Alger in HMS *Dorsetshire*. The British knew that the commerce raiders had been in the area earlier during the year and expected a return trip. But the real reason for so much action was to assure the safety of troop convoys bound for North Africa and Malaya via the Cape of Good Hope. Putting himself in the position of the enemy, Admiral Willis assumed that they would soon launch a U-boat campaign against the South Atlantic, and he undertook to hit the U-boats and the raiders where it hurt—by taking their supply ships. Knowing the South Atlantic Ocean and the calm spots where ships would normally seek sanctuary for rendezvous and refueling, the British had a good idea of where to look for Germans.

On the morning of November 22, Captain R. D. Oliver of the Royal Navy was taking his heavy cruiser *Devonshire* through the waters of the South Atlantic, very near to the equator. HMS *Devonshire* was a stout ship, built in 1929, with a displacement of 9,850 tons, an armament of eight 8-inch guns and eight 4-inch guns. She carried observation aircraft, and she had a speed of 32 knots. She was, in effect, a ship built for battle with other ships-of-the-line, but that was not her task on November 22. She was killing rats, so to speak.

On the morning of November 22, the *Devonshire* launched her Walrus observation plane on the regular dawn reconnaissance mission. As always, radio silence was observed by the plane, and when it had flown its pattern it returned to the cruiser to report having sighted one merchant ship 4° 21′ South, 18° 50′ West. The captain was informed, and he ordered the ship's course changed to close with the merchantman at 25 knots.

Shortly after dawn on this November 22, the lookouts on *Raider 16* reported sighting the long, gray shape of the surfaced German U-boat. She finally came gliding up to *Raider 16*, and out of her conning tower climbed a succession of lean, bearded young men who waved and cheered the ship as they came on. It was a fresh morning with some scattered clouds in the sky, the wind was blowing at Force 4, which gave the ships some sea to contend with and a visibility of about 10 miles around.

Raider 16 stopped and launched her big motorboat to pick up Kapitänleutnant Bauer and several of his men. They came back to the ship to make known their needs, and the fuel lines were snaked out on the raider and readied to go over the stern. Soon the lines were made fast, and *U-126* began sucking fuel from the ship.

Kapitänleutnant Bauer and his officers stepped into the wardroom where Captain Rogge was frankly ready to impress them. He had the tables laid with white cloths amd gleaming silver, and waiters hovered about with napkins on their arms. The menu included ham and eggs and half a dozen other delicacies that the U-boat men had not seen for a long time.

Before they sat down for a glass of sherry, Chief Engineer Kielhorn came up out of the engine room to report a defect in the port engine. He wanted to repair it right then, while the ship was lying quiet.

Captain Rogge acceded to the engineer's wishes, even though it meant some down time for changing a piston in one of the cylinders. But he wanted Kielhorn to make all haste, for he admitted that he did not at all like the idea of lying half disabled at this rendezvous in the South Atlantic. The Pacific and the Indian Oceans were much to be preferred to the South Atlantic; it was too narrow and there were too many British cruisers in the region these days.

Bauer and Rogge sat down to eat, and Bauer wolfed his food while Rogge plied him with questions about the Europe the U-boat commander had left just a few weeks before. Surgeon Reil and Surgeon Sprung came into the wardroom, pulled up chairs, and joined the festivities.

In his cabin, Adjutant Mohr was sweating in the toils of a nightmare that had been troubling him for six months. Each morning or night before he awoke he dreamed that he saw an enemy cruiser bearing 20 degrees to port, not an auxiliary cruiser but a real warship, with three funnels and turrets, and just as he awakened each time he had the sinking sensation that the end had come. Then, invariably, Mohr would wake up.

Rogge had been joking with Mohr about the dream all these months. As the adjutant awoke cold and sweaty, he knew his captain would joke with him again this day. He washed his face, shaved, dressed in a clean duty uniform, and went on deck. From the wardroom he could hear the laughing and talk of those inside. He paused for a moment, then mounted to the bridge and spoke to the officer of the watch. Rogge was doing the honors. His place was up here. He looked around; all seemed to be shipshape, and from the deck forward he caught a snatch of song—the *Atlantis* men off watch were entertaining the seamen from the U-boat, as they ought to be doing.

In the wardroom, breakfast was soon enough finished and the officers sat back to enjoy their coffee and talk about the war. On the bridge the officer of the watch grinned at Adjutant Mohr.

"Thank God yesterday's panic is over . . ."

He was referring to the accident in which the seaplane had been so badly damaged. The disconsolate Flying Officer Bulla was regarding the hook of the seaplane hoist with distaste, and mourning the virtual death of his first Arado airplane.

"Oh well, it can't be helped," said Mohr philosophically. He knew that Rogge was distressed by the loss of the airplane just at a time when they needed her extra eyes. "A lot more peaceful now," he said.

Adjutant Mohr then turned his attention to the sea that lapped about them grayly in the cloudy morning. He ducked inside for a moment and got a mug of coffee which he brought back to the bridge. The coffee tasted so good that it overcame the reek of fuel oil drifting upward from the stern. The ship lolled in the gentle sea, and the breeze across the decks was just enough to stimulate.

Aboard HMS *Devonshire* the executive officer was questioning the pilot of the Walrus airplane about what he had seen, and the more he questioned, the more suspicious he became that the "merchant ship" was one of the German raiders which had been harrying shipping in the region for so long.

In the cruiser's tall masts, the lookouts sang out at 08:09 to announce the sighting of masts almost dead ahead.

Six minutes passed. On *Raider 16*, in the wardroom below, Kapitänleutnant Bauer was talking to Captain Rogge about taking a real bath! The surgeons were discussing the improvement in quality of the whiskey since Dr. Reil had begun distilling his own water and adding a touch of seawater to flavor it—something like a high-grade mineral spring effect had been achieved. On the stern, the men in charge of oiling waited patiently as the fuel ran through the hoses. On the U-boat, the first lieutenant and the men were on war watch—not at action stations but wary and ready as they always must be when on the surface and out of a friendly port.

At 08:16 came a hail from the raider's lookout in the foremast.

"Three-funneled ship bearing red two zero."

On the bridge the klaxon sounded and the alarm bells began to sing out. On the stern the lines were cast off, and the fuel pipe was capped. On the U-boat men began piling down the conning tower.

Captain Rogge rushed to his bridge from the wardroom, Kapitänleutnant Bauer on his heels, both struggled into lifejackets, as did every other man, automatically, the result of months of habit.

Captain Rogge picked up the voice pipe to the engine room.

"*Volle voraus!*" he shouted. Full speed ahead!

He instructed the chief engineer to start the port engine as quickly as he could and give full power. He ordered the helmsman to turn hard aport to show his stern to the enemy and keep her from identifying the ship if she had not—also to give the smallest possible target, and to hide the U-boat.

He need not have worried about the U-boat.

"Bastards . . . bloody bastards," shouted Kapitänleutnant Bauer, who was anxiously dancing about the deck, furious at being stuck on this fat ship when he should be in command of his U-boat. As they watched, the U-boat crash-dived.

"To dive like that when she couldn't even SEE the enemy!" Bauer said. He shook his head and subsided in woe.

But in a moment Bauer saw why the U-boat had dived so quickly, and anyone must agree that his executive officer had been wise to take her down. There, flying in broad circles, was the fat, awkward form of the *Devonshire*'s Walrus airplane, sitting like a huge bumblebee up in the air, its pilot making slow turns, its observer watching and taking pictures of the ship below.

"Give the swine a burst," shouted a seaman.

Rogge glared. He looked off at the ship coming toward him and even at this narrow angle he could recognize her as one of the class of *Dorsetshire*, for he had berthed alongside her in Hong Kong when he was first officer of the cruiser *Karlsruhe* in 1936.

Had the pilot seen the submarine?

He must have seen the hosepipe which was lying in the water. He must have seen the raider's motorboat, which had been tied up to the submarine until a few moments before.

The answer came soon enough.

"Aircraft is signaling SSS . . . SSS . . . SSS with his signal lamp."

The Walrus *had* seen the submarine, and was warning the cruiser not to come closer lest she take a torpedo.

Up in the Walrus, the observer was making careful comparison of the ship beneath him and a number of photographs. Most telling of these photographs was one taken from *Life* magazine on the capture of *ZamZam*. David Scherman, the *Life* photographer, had struck up an acquaintance with Adjutant Mohr, who was an enthusiastic amateur photographer and had the highest respect for the professional. Mohr had let Scherman have the run of the raider for photo purposes, knowing it could hurt nothing to let him take people and interior shots, but making sure that Scherman got no pictures of the ship's silhouette or camouflage. Then, when the passengers of *ZamZam* had been disembarked from *Dresden* on arrival in France, the authorities had made sure that they took away most of Scherman's interior shots—and had somehow left him with telltale pictures of the silhouette of *Atlantis*, taken either from the sinking *ZamZam* as she was attacked, or from the *Dresden* as she pulled away, but pictures that the men of the raider did not know Scherman had taken.

The observer and the pilot conferred. The appearance of this ship certainly resembled the description of the *Raider 16* given in the supplement of the Weekly Intelligence Report No. 64, and in that issue of *Life* for June 23, 1941. One could discount ventilators, deckhouses, samson posts, and such minor variables. What was important was the general configuration and the shape of the hull.

On receiving the signal that warned of the submarine, the big cruiser sheered away and began zigzagging, remaining between 18,000 and 12,000 yards away from the raider, at a speed of 26 knots. She made a difficult target as she danced about.

On *Raider 16*, Captain Rogge kept his eyes glued to his glasses, except to raise his head once in a while and observe the buzzing bee that was the Walrus above them.

Kasch wanted to start shooting, if not at the plane then at the ship.

Captain Rogge ordered him to hold his fire.

The ship's motor launch finally got under way and came rushing back like a frightened duckling. Otherwise there was silence except for the droning of the plane above and the throbbing of *Raider 16*'s engine.

Rogge called his officers around him, and calmly told them that they would play for time. "We'll pretend that we are British," he said. If the cruiser then came in close, the submarine should be able to slam a torpedo into her—at least there was that chance, and a chance was better than none. Even *Raider 16* might try a torpedo—and if they had never worked accurately before, perhaps they would in this hour of need.

"We've got the U-boat," said Rogge, and he warned that not a gun was to be exposed, not a movement made that might appear suspicious to the airplane.

CHAPTER TWENTY-SIX

Vengeance

Aboard the *Devonshire* Captain Oliver was taking it slow and easy in the best tradition of the British navy. His Walrus had signaled to warn of the danger of a submarine, but he did not know precisely what evidence the Walrus had found, since the plane was maintaining radio silence. He was cautious enough to circle the suspect ship like a boxer circling his foe, but he was not going to open fire on what might be a harmless merchantman, much as he suspected she was anything but harmless. Also, he was concerned lest there be British prisoners of war on the ship.

Yet something must be done. So, at 08:37, the captain gave the order to the gunnery officer to fire two salvos, to right and left of the ship.

From the decks of *Raider 16*, *Devonshire* was a beautiful, frightening sight as she sped along circling and dodging. Then came a flash from the cruiser, and less than half a minute later the splashes of a salvo over the ship and off the bow. Flash-flash—crash-crash—and splash-splash off the stern.

The meaning was unmistakable to Rogge, who had fired over other vessels so many times before in the past year and a half. He had been bracketed. He was warned.

"Eight-inch guns!" said someone in awe, and a wag among the crowd offered the thought that it was better to give than to receive.

Rogge ordered the ship turned to the south-southwest.

"Stop engines," he ordered. "Hard aport. Let him see that we are hove to."

He meant engine, not engines, for at best, even with the

167

expert mechanics of *Raider 16*, it would have taken four hours down time to repair the disassembled engine, and it simply could not be put in service on short notice. With one engine she might make 10 knots, and they had already seen the cruiser making nearly 30.

Seeing that there was no escape, Captain Rogge decided to bluff. Up went the flag signaling, "I am stopped," and his radio officer began transmitting a signal:

"RRR . . . RRR . . . RRR . . . *Polyphemus* 4° 21' South, 18° 15' West . . . RRR . . . RRR . . . RRR . . . *Polyphemus* . . ."

If only the cruiser would come in close, and if only *U-126* would take a shot at her—that was the thought uppermost in Rogge's mind.

Alas—under the guidance of the inexperienced first officer, *U-126* had dived deep when she felt those first salvos strike the water. But she was to come up again, and watch . . .

The Walrus began to signal *Raider 16*.

"N . . . N . . . J . . . N . . . N . . . J—What ship?"

On the deck Rogge ordered his sailors to wave at the Walrus, as though the airplane and the cruiser were the best friends they had in the world.

The signalman on the bridge of the raider looked at the captain.

"What shall I reply, sir?"

Rogge told him to acknowledge the message slowly and ask that it be repeated.

"The ship's signaling now, too," said the radio shack.

Rogge gave the same instructions.

So the signalman answered the British by lamp and by radio, identifying the raider as *Polyphemus*, a Dutch freighter that had left Spain some time ago, and might possibly be in these waters.

The ruse might have worked, except for one thing: in all the months at sea, the Germans had heard distress calls innumerable times but they had still not mastered the art of sending them. Aboard the *Devonshire* Captain Oliver and his communications officer consulted over the words coming from this supposed Dutch freighter, and came to some tentative conclusions.

No signal letters were included, as would have been done by any legitimate freighter that knew the merchant code.

But then, in times of stress these merchantmen did strange

things with their wireless, and every British naval officer who had to deal with freighters or convoys knew that well.

But it was even more suspicious that the R's were transmitted in groups of three—the German fashion—and not in groups of four as the British had been doing since the war's beginning.

Still, Captain Oliver must consider the possibility that he was shooting at an innocent Allied ship.

An Admiralty message of October 22 had indicated that the *Polyphemus* was in Balboa, Canal Zone, on September 21. Where might she be now? It *was* possible that she could be in the South Atlantic, if no one else knew where.

Captain Oliver sent a quick message to the commander in chief, South Atlantic.

"Is *Polyphemus* genuine?"

Meanwhile, the airplane and the cruiser were in touch, and Captain Oliver asked the essential question:

"What type of stern has she got?"

"Cruiser stern hull similar to *Atlantis*," was the reply.

Then came a reply from the commander in chief, Atlantic, to the question about *Polyphemus*'s genuineness in these waters.

"No. Repeat, no."

Captain Oliver had all the information he needed!

He continued to zigzag. He continued to stay outside the 16,000-yard range, which put him far beyond the reach of *Raider 16*'s 150 mm. guns.

On the bridge of *Raider 16*, Captain Rogge stood with his staff around him. Lieutenant Kasch was there, aching to start shooting at something. Lieutenant Fehler was there, hoping to use a torpedo. Navigator Kamenz was there, and so was Adjutant Mohr. Behind them stood three torpedo men, three gunners, three signalmen, and a rangefinder. And with them all was Kapitänleutnant Bauer, the most helpless of the lot, pacing up and down the length of the bridge, becoming even more angry at the failure of *U-126* to make her presence known.

It was 09:34 when the commander in chief, South Atlantic, replied to *Devonshire*'s question about the *Polyphemus*.

On the raider Rogge was speaking.

"She will find that we are not *Polyphemus*, of course," he said. "Then we can expect her to be *really* rude. Even so, I'm not going to fire."

Gunnery Officer Kasch was shocked. Not fire?

But he knew that they were out of range. He knew that if by some miracle *Devonshire* slipped into range and he hit her with a complete salvo on deck, those 150 mm. shells would still bounce right off the armor plating of the heavy cruiser.

"A shell or two?" asked Kasch. "Just for the sake of prestige?"

"No," said Rogge. He still hoped to bluff the enemy. If *Devonshire* began firing, and *Raider 16* did not fire back, there was still the chance they might take her for a supply ship and leave her alone, or close in, and give the torpedo men of *Raider 16* and the submarine a chance.

Then it was 09:35.

Devonshire began firing.

The first salvo struck short, sending huge gouts of foaming water into the air.

The second salvo straddled the raider, and a splinter struck the foredeck.

Captain Rogge turned hard astarboard and ordered the engine room to make smoke to screen the ship.

Before the ship could actually turn, the third salvo struck, one shell exploding on the hangar deck, knocking out several of the electrical circuits and setting fire to the seaplane.

Then the internal telephones failed.

The radio station lost its power.

Captain Rogge ordered the auxiliary system plugged in, but it was so weak that not enough power could be generated to send a message to Berlin. The electrical circuits to the boat davits failed, and when Rogge ordered the men into boats, they had to be cranked down by hand.

Mohr stood next to his commander on the bridge, feeling and looking gray. His batman came up and offered him "his best uniform."

He was startled, but he went below and put it on. He also secured some dollar currency that the administrative officer kept in the safe for emergency use, and put it in his shoes.

The other officers went about their business, all but Kapitän-leutnant Bauer, who had no business, because his U-boat had disappeared. What he did not know was that his first lieutenant was sitting down below at 300 feet, waiting. It would have made no difference the way *Devonshire* played the game, but it infuriated the U-boat captain.

Oberleutnant Kasch lounged on the rail and counted the intervals. He saw a flash.

"They'll be here in twenty seconds," he said, coolly, looking at his watch.

The smoke began to take effect, and the ship had some respite as the salvos fell in the water around her. There was time to get the men into the boats, and that was all that concerned Captain Rogge.

Captain Oliver stopped firing and altered his course to get clear of the smoke. He tried his radar fire control mechanism, but it was not very successful.

Rogge was now frantically clearing his ship. All the boats and rafts were in the water, including two cutters that had no davits—so efficient was this crew of *Raider 16* even in a moment of despair.

It was 09:43. The *Devonshire* had circled around until she was in a position where she could see *Raider 16* again and she reopened fire.

The raider began taking hits again.

Captain Rogge handed his little dog Ferry to one of the sailors and the dog went into a boat. Adjutant Mohr went down to his cabin to throw the codes overboard in a weighted bag, and picked up his camera and film.

By the time he reappeared on deck, *Raider 16* had taken eight hits and her whole configuration had changed. The ventilators were broken and twisted. The derricks were collapsed. The smell of fire hung heavy over her, and black smoke rose to her masthead. The seaplane hangar was raging with flames, and a dozen small fires could be seen along the decks.

By this time the crew was off the ship. All who remained aboard were Captain Rogge, Chief Petty Officer Pigors, Leutnant Fehler and his demolition party, and Adjutant Mohr.

Mohr slipped as he walked the deck—blood. Seven men had died and First Officer Kühn had been wounded by a splinter but had been put into a boat.

Rogge told Fehler to set his charges and leave. He ordered the others off the bridge, but he lingered himself. Neither Chief Petty Officer Pigors nor Mohr would go.

Rogge was musing to himself.

The boats were away.

The scuttling charges began to go off in the engine room.

The ship took a definite list to port and began to go down by the stern. Anyone who was abandoning ship had best do so now.

Still Rogge lingered.

Had he done his best? he asked.

Could he face Berlin?

Should he do as had Captain Hans Langsdorf of the *Graf Spee*, who shot himself when he lost his ship through no fault of his own?

Could he return to Hitler's Germany?

Rogge was considering these matters, as Mohr destroyed the last of the papers and Chief Petty Officer Pigors came up.

"It's time to leave, sir," said Pigors.

Rogge shouted something but nothing could be heard above the shooting until they moved to the other side of the ship. Pigors was insistent.

"There's no sense in staying here, sir," he said. "There's nothing more you can do. But the men out there need you."

Rogge shook his head. He told Pigors to leave him.

"No," said the petty officer. "If you don't come with me, sir, I'll stay here too."

Fehler and his men were swarming over the side. Rogge, Mohr, and Pigors now jumped.

They were just in time. Five more salvos came over quickly, and one caught a magazine, which went up in flames.

On the forecastle there suddenly appeared one lone man. He had been below, at a telephone station, and receiving no answer to his calls he had remained at his post as trained to do. Now he had felt the trembling and changing of the ship and had come on deck. He looked around and jumped.

All the men near the ship watched the stern, and all of them began to swim for dear life away from the suction they knew was coming.

The hit on the magazine came at 10:02, and that ended the firing for *Devonshire*. From his bridge Captain Oliver could see that it would not be necessary to send another shell into the hulk, for it was a matter of minutes before her life was snuffed out.

The men of the *Raider 16* struggled in the water, moving away from the stricken ship and away from the cruiser. Captain Oliver knew they were there, and although he was tempted to try to rescue survivors, the safety of his ship came first. There was no question in his mind about the presence of a submarine in the area. He sat by and watched; he had done what he could to preserve life by fusing his shells at the base instead of at the nose. Several men in the water were killed by near misses but not nearly so many as would have died had the shells been nose-fused.

But that was the only concession Captain Oliver felt it proper to make. The raider, which had dealt death and destruction to 22 ships, was now feeling the taste of death in her own throat.

Devonshire stood by, waiting. At 10:14 came another explosion from deep inside the hulk—the last of the scuttling charges—and *Raider 16* sank, stern first, at 10:16.

In the water, in the middle of a crowd of twenty swimming men, Captain Rogge drew himself upright and trod water. His hand raised to his forehead in salute as his ship sank and Mohr, who was right beside him, saw that his commander was crying.

CHAPTER TWENTY-SEVEN

The Rescue

Captain Oliver gave an order, and HMS *Devonshire* swung off to the northwest. She headed back toward the position in which she had found herself early in the morning, stopping at 10:40 to pick up the Walrus which had done her job for the war if she never flew again. Then the British cruiser disappeared over the horizon, leaving more than 300 Germans and 1 American survivor* in boats and rafts, clinging to their sides, or swimming toward the cluster. Captain Rogge knew their position, 4° 20′ South, 18° 35′ West. He began rallying the men, and got them to give three cheers for their sunken ship. Then they headed with his encouragement toward the string of boats.

Captain Oliver had some bad moments now. After he had signaled South Atlantic Headquarters and the commander in chief had indicated that *Polyphemus* could not be genuine, somebody at headquarters had second thoughts. *Devonshire* opened fire on the raider, but afterward learned that headquarters was sending messages all over the Atlantic in search of the real *Polyphemus*. It was not until next day that the Dutch ship was located in New York Harbor and Captain Oliver could heave a very real sigh of relief from responsibility for having fired first and investigated not at all.

During the last stages of the uneven battle, *U-126* had come to periscope depth and was hoping that *Devonshire* might come in close enough for a torpedo shot, but Captain Oliver was too wary. . When the heavy cruiser steamed out of sight, the U-boat came to the surface and moved toward the rafts and boats.

---

*The prisoner, Frank Vicovari, had been badly wounded during the *ZamZam* affair and had been kept by *Raider 16* for medical treatment. He survived.

Captain Rogge quickly made his way to one of the boats and got in. The bosun followed him and began piping for the attention of the men of *Raider 16*.

The captain stood up and cupped his hands.

"All boats gather round me," he shouted.

The men had been struggling aimlessly in the water. Sharks circled round them but contented themselves with feasting on the dead and did not touch the living. One by one the men were pulled into the boats and rafts. There was no room for some, so the men in the boats began building rafts from the wreckage floating around them.

Adjutant Mohr swam and clung to the sides of boats for two hours before he was hauled into one of the whalers assembling around Captain Rogge. By this time all the men were somehow accommodated out of the water, and the captain could put his mind to the plans needed for their salvation.

Meanwhile the men sat numbly. Mohr looked around for Helmsman Kross, his companion on two dozen boarding expeditions. Kross was dead, killed by a shell bursting on the companionway to the boat deck. Some, like First Officer Kühn, had been wounded, and some were scratched and cut and shocked. The surgeons were already at work in the boats, treating the worst cases.

There were 60 men in Mohr's boat, squatting and sitting and lying along the gunwales. The boats floated among the wreckage left from the ship, and Flying Officer Bulla suddenly recognized his chest of drawers. It was dragged to the side of the boat, and he calmly sat there, pulling out items he thought he might need and stuffing them in his pockets. The other things were shared out, and the chest was then dropped back into the sea to drift slowly away.

It was some time before the captain could assemble all the boats around him. Then up came the steel cutters, motorboats, and five rubber boats.

By noon all men were safe and the boats had their oars out and were rowing. The U-boat came alongside and took Kapitän-leutnant Bauer, all the wounded, and the men on the rubber boats.

Captain Rogge counted heads, and then called the roll. Surprisingly enough, only seven men of the whole crew were missing. He then announced his plans. Besides the wounded, the specialists from the ship's company were to be embarked on the submarine; they were of most value to the Fatherland and it was most important that they survive. So 10 officers, 6 chief petty officers, 16 petty officers, and 23 sailors were taken aboard the submarine. The rest of the men were assigned to the two motorboats and four steel cutters, each boat commanded by an officer, and the boats taken in tow. There were still too many men, so 52 men in lifejackets were placed aboard the deck of the submarine with instructions that if she dived, they were to make for the boats and hang on until the submarine returned.

All was assembled.

When the U-boat had appeared, Kapitänleutnant Bauer was quite beside himself; his poor first officer stuck his head out of the conning tower expecting to be greeted like a rescuing angel, and was thoroughly tonguelashed by Bauer for not having attacked the cruiser. Rogge intervened, however, pointing out that the cruiser had behaved very properly and cautiously and that the youngster could not have done more than he did except to risk sinking—and then where would they all be?

The officers held a conference regarding their course. They could set course for Freetown, heading for the main trade routes and making use of the generally eastern currents in this region. Or they could head for Brazil, which was 900 miles away.

Rogge did not like the first plan, for it meant that almost certainly the men of *Raider 16* would spend the rest of the war as prisoners. The Germans from the *Graf Spee* helped settle the matter, for they had been interned by local authorities in Montevideo, had escaped, and had spent several months living in the countryside, being passed along from one German farm to another until finally they had been smuggled onto the blockade runner and come to sea—to join *Raider 16* and fight again.

This story, and this ideal, appealed to Rogge and his men, and with lighter hearts, then, they opted to attempt the 900-mile voyage to the Brazilian coast.

So they set off, at four o'clock that afternoon, the boats waggling slowly on the end of the slow tow. Mohr dried his precious dollars in the sun, and his spirits rose with the thought of freedom. It was to be a twelve-day cruise to Brazil, then!

U-126 sent a report to Berlin.

"*Ship 16* sunk by English 10,000-ton cruiser. Am trying to reach South America coast with lifeboats and 305 men. Oil replenishment absolutely essential."

So they cruised, at 7 knots, keeping a nervous eye peeled for smoke or the sight of a mast anywhere on the horizon, and for the first time since setting out to sea 21 months before, the men of *Raider 16* hoped not to see any smoke.

On they cruised, in fine weather with a following sea that helped keep up their speed. But the yawing of the motorboats put heavy strain on the rope hawsers, and from time to time the convoy stopped while the ropes were mended. Then the pressure of towing began to act on the wooden planks of the motorboats and they kept filling with water, so they had to be bailed.

In the morning the sun came up—not an unmixed blessing to men in open boats, who had spent enough time in the water to have their clothing thoroughly saturated. The salt dried in the clothes and rubbed raw spots on their skin. Cuts and scratches became infected, and lips and eyes began to swell. The decks of the boats and submarine grew so hot it was torture to lie on a place that had been in the sun, and the men tore up strips of cloth to cover their feet against the contact. Mohr was lucky— to save his money he had worn his shoes, and he was one of the few men in the boats with shoes on.

By day they roasted and bailed and rowed to catch up when the towlines broke. By night they froze, huddling together for what warmth that brought.

At noon on November 23, Captain Rogge and Kapitänleutnant Bauer made some estimates by dead reckoning, and figured that they had covered 150 of the miles from their point of departure to Pernambuco. It would be only five or six days rather than a dozen. Rogge looked around at his men in the boats and was thankful. If the supply of towlines held . . .

There was little to eat in the boats—only the supply of biscuit and water that each boat carried could be doled out for the first meal or so. Then the submarine managed to give extra food to each of the boats—but the strain of more than 300 extra mouths told on the submarine, too.

Along about evening on the second day out, Kapitänleutnant Bauer's radio operators caught a signal from Berlin. It was welcome news: the German Admiralty had ordered three U-boats and the supply ship *Python* to come to the aid of the sunken mariners. And 76 hours after they set out from that little point in the ocean, *Python* came up. They were saved.

CHAPTER TWENTY-EIGHT

The Python Adventure

Python was one of the U-boat supply ships sent out late in October, 1941, from France to underwrite the new line of aggressive submarine warfare in the South Atlantic. She had been assigned to accompany and supply the boats *UA, U-124*, and *U-129*. She was really as much U-boat tender as supply ship, with her big superstructure and heavy cranes and vast storage capacities. She was to be the U-boats' home away from home.

When Berlin learned, however, that *Atlantis* had been sunk, *Python* was diverted for the rescue task, and at dawn on November 24 she found the little flotilla. As she came alongside, some of the sailors of *Python* leaned over the side and made jokes with the survivors of the raider. Rogge came up the conning tower of the submarine, dressed in officer's cap and jacket, shorts and tennis shoes, and climbed up to the deck of the rescue ship, saluted, and addressed himself to the captain.

"I report myself and the crew of the auxiliary cruiser *Atlantis*, aboard *Python*."

Then it was all over. The boats were being hoisted in, the men of *Raider 16* were going below and getting baths and soap and borrowed clothes from their countrymen. Captain Rogge was given a cabin—one he had once occupied when this ship was a fruit liner. Mohr and two other *Atlantis* officers shared a luxurious suite—cabin and stateroom. That first night they had a huge meal in the wardroom, washed down with brandy and coffee, and Captain Rogge went below to see how his men were faring. There was not enough room in the forecastle for the men of *Raider 16*, but there was plenty of room in the holds and there were plenty of mattresses so they could stretch out in

178

comfort. There was good food, potatoes and fresh fruit, and the men were as happy as might be expected.

While the officers and men of *Raider 16* enjoyed themselves, rested, and congratulated one another on their salvation, *Python* refueled *U-126* and replaced the provisions which had been devoured by the rescued during the three-day trek across the open sea.

Rogge mused on the course of events. He had traveled 102,000 miles in 622 days at sea. His ship had sunk or captured 22 ships totaling 145,000 tons of shipping—more than any other German ship. He had succeeded completely in his mission. Had he stuck to his mission and gone home at the end of it, he might be standing on his own bridge at this moment—what had brought about disaster was the voluntary supply operation which was not included in his operational orders. That fact hurt, and it hurt as much that he had let *Raider 16* go down without a fight. And yet, although Rogge did not know it, even in the sinking of the *Raider 16* he had achieved a kind of triumph because Captain Oliver never did know what he had sunk, and he left the area believing it was one of the U-boat supply ships like *Python*. So the British continued to search the waters of the South Atlantic and the Indian Ocean for *Raider 16* for several weeks, while she lay deep on the bottom of the sea and her crew rode the ocean.

Rogge was tortured by the memory of the decisions he had made on the day that his ship was lost. It had been his invariable rule, when meeting with another ship, to assume that the enemy had DF'd their radio transmissions, and accordingly to run at least 200 miles in another direction with the other ship before stopping and exchanging supplies. He had violated his own rule on November 22 for the first and last time. Was he justified simply because his port engine needed work? He *could* have steamed along on the starboard engine alone. Or would it have made the slightest difference, given the *Devonshire* and her Walrus aircraft?

Such useless speculation occupied many hours of Rogge's time for several days, until he received a message from Grossadmiral Raeder himself, approving Rogge's action in saving his crew and allowing *Raider 16* to be sunk without a fight when she was overwhelmed by the British cruiser. His conscience was eased, and he was certain that his career was saved.

Berlin was also busy planning *Python*'s schedule. She was to refuel *UA, U-68, U-124*, and *U-129* within a week, beginning on November 30, and then return to France where the crew of *Raider 16* could be landed safely.

So *Python* steamed to 27° 53′ South, 3° 55′ West, and here on the evening of November 30 she met *U-68*. It was just about two weeks since Korvettenkapitän Merten had walked the deck of *Atlantis* as his boat was refueled from the raider. How things had changed! As soon as *U-68* came alongside, the supply operation began even though a heavy swell was running. *UA* was supposed to come in at the same time but she was delayed and did not arrive until the next day. Consequently, *Python* lay rolling gently in the swell all day long and was still in the same place at 15:30 that afternoon of December 1, as the shadows began to fall and the cool breeze kept the full force of the sun from the half-naked men of the supply ship busy moving food and clothing and engine room equipment aboard the two submarines.

The men of *Raider 16* had no responsibility. They lounged on deck, gazing idly at the working parties, or they stayed below and napped or read or played cards.

Mohr was asleep in his bunk, glad of the respite after nearly two years of constantly alert duty. Rogge was restless and had stepped to the bridge, because he was happier on a bridge than anywhere else. It was 15:30 exactly.

"*Ein Fahrzeug mit drei Schornsteinen . . .*" said one of the men of *Raider 16* who was in the foremast just to help out—the lookout of *Python*, who was six feet higher in the crow's nest, had not even seen it. It was a battle cruiser, about 19 miles away.

It did not matter that *Python*'s man had been caught napping. The three-funneled ship was coming down on them too quickly.

On the supply ship, the lines were hauled in, the fuel caps replaced, and the rubber boats and fuel lines with which they had been working were cast off. *Python* revved up to full speed and headed northeast. The alarm bells clanged shrilly throughout the ship.

Inside the ship, doors thudded open and closed, boots began pounding up and down the corridors. Mohr awoke abruptly from a pleasant dream and moved toward the bridge, wondering what it was all about.

Then he heard the cry that had rung through *Raider 16* nine days earlier.

"*Feindlicher Kreuzer in Sicht!*"—Enemy cruiser in sight!

Then Mohr heard more orders.

"Oil pipe free."

"Full ahead."

Indeed, as Rogge observed with some dismay, they were going full ahead, so much so that they were making sparks and thick black smoke that tipped the enemy off at the moment that they were running away. .

But what difference would that have made?

The ship bearing down on them was HMS *Dorsetshire*, sistership of the *Devonshire*, hunting German supply ships and submarines in these waters. At 16:33 her Walrus airplane had sighted the masts of a ship about 18 miles away—just after Rogge's eagle-eyed lookout had seen the cruiser—and immediately the *Dorsetshire* began moving in at a speed of 30 knots.

At 17:08 several small oil patches were sighted from the cruiser's aircraft, which indicated that the ship had been refueling something. Since only one hull had been seen, it was natural for Captain Alger to assume that the ship had been refueling submarines, and he turned away to avoid possible U-boat attack.

No torpedo tracks were seen, and for good reason.

As the klaxons sounded in the German supply ship and in the submarines, *UA* dived quickly and deeply to escape. *U-68* had been busy shipping torpedoes and stowing them, and they were not properly put away at this moment—which meant this ship's trim was all wrong. *U-68* dived, and shot down, almost straight down, so fast that she was able to recover only by taking the strongest measures.

By the time *U-68* was able to surface for a shot, she was out of position. At 3,000 yards *UA* fired five torpedoes, but Captain Alger was on the alert, he zigzagged constantly in his approach, and came no closer than 16,000 yards to the *Python*.

Dorsetshire approached at 25 knots, zigzagging, and Captain Alger noticed that the other ship was making quite a bit of smoke. He sighted the *Python*'s boats with dinghies in tow, and thought at first he had seen the conning tower of a U-boat.

Was this ship ahead of him a German? Or was she a frightened merchantman who had just had a narrow escape from a submarine?

The cruiser came up, fired a shot to each side of the supply ship, and then observed white smoke coming from the stern of the ship. Captain Alger decided to stay outside a range of 8 miles, just to be sure he did not receive return fire from what might be a raider. He was quite right in being suspicious. The captain of the *Python* was furious with his crew, for he was trying to play the part of the innocent and someone had mistakenly turned on the after smoke-making rig.

Captain Alger stood off, zigzagging. Aboard *Python* came the order to abandon ship and scuttle. The boats were put over the side, and this action was seen from the cruiser. The captain said that perhaps some English prisoners were aboard the ship and so he would give all the time in the world for the boats to get away lest they be hit by shellfire.

At 17:51 the bridge began to blaze from fires set by the scuttling party. Korvettenkapitän Lueders, of the *Python*, stayed on deck, along with his scuttling party and the indefatigable explosives man, Leutnant Fehler. They placed the scuttling charges in the holds while most of the boats pulled away.

Fortunately for the crews of *Python* and *Raider 16*, they had taken aboard all the boats from the raider. Fortunately, also, when the cruiser appeared, the crew of *Python* had been making ready to supply *U-68* with food and it was neatly stacked on deck. It was not a great matter to put this food supply into the boats as they went over the side. At least the men of the ships could eat while shipwrecked.

At 18:05 *Python* was burning merrily, and soon there was an explosion from below. The demolition men, assisted by Leutnant Fehler, had sprinkled gasoline around below. At 18:21 there was a large explosion forward and *Python* went down, leaving a trail of smoke in the air. Every man had gotten off.

Dorsetshire wasted little time in the area, but headed off south, while her Walrus came circling over, estimated that the men in the boats numbered 500, and went back to the cruiser. Her captain was puzzled by the presence of so many men aboard the German ship, and attributed it to spare crews for U-boats.

In the water were eleven ship's boats and seven rubber boats, holding 414 survivors from *Python* and *Raider 16*. Two submarines were somewhere about them for protection, but they were estimated to be 5,000 miles from Germany.

Home had never seemed so far away.

CHAPTER TWENTY-NINE

The Long Voyage

Not long after the *Dorsetshire* steamed off south, *UA* surfaced, and Captain Eckermann told the story of his attack. *Dorsetshire* had zigzagged so successfully and changed her speed so quickly that he had quite misjudged her and his two spreads of torpedoes were not even close. It was a miserable affair. Soon they were joined by Korvettenkapitän Merten in *U-68* and the four ship captains met to decide the best way they might hope to get these 400 men back to German territory.

The task that faced the Germans was certainly not easy. The British had very nearly swept the South Atlantic clear of German ships of all kinds but submarines. The day of the surface raider was very nearly over, as the figures showed. Between the beginning of war and the end of 1941, warship raiders had sunk or captured 59 Allied vessels, totaling 331,692 tons. In the same period, the merchant raiders had sunk or captured 98 ships with a total of 593,201 tons. Of the seven numbered raiders, four had returned safely to Germany. *Raider 33* (*Pinguin*) was sunk May 8, 1941. *Raider 41* (*Kormoran*) was sunk a few days before *Atlantis*, in a battle with the light cruiser *Sydney*, which also went down. The raiders had comported themselves well and justifed their existence, but like the U-boat supply ships, they simply could not stand up forever against constant British vigilance. And what was happening to the survivors of *Raider 16* and *Python* now was that there simply was not anyone in the South Atlantic to take them home except the submarines.

By far the easiest solution would be to make for land and either try to conduct guerrilla operations or give themselves up.

Captain Rogge had no such intention.

The very first matter that concerned him was the establishment of command. Commander Eckermann, the young man in charge of U-boat *UA*, attempted to claim that he was senior officer present because he was senior officer in charge of an operational ship. Between them, however, Rogge and Commander Merten managed to convince the ebullient Eckermann that Berlin might take a very strong view of his assumption of such authority with a full-fledged Kapitän zur See and a national hero, which Rogge was by this time, unwillingly under his command. Commander Eckermann was overruled, and Captain Rogge in *U-68* became admiral of the little fleet.

The plan was then worked out.

Each U-boat took a hundred men below, where they tried to stay out of the way of the crews. The rubber boats were then taken aboard the U-boat decks to save wear and tear. The U-boats each took five lifeboats in tow, and the *Atlantis*'s motor launch, information, and messages from the submarines to the lifeboats.

Life in the boats was grim, as told by Adjutant Mohr in his recollections ten years later.*

"You'll die like rats in a trap," he screamed. "You'll die slowly . . . slowly I tell you!"

The frenzied cry, the words tumbling over each other, cut through my half doze, waking me again to the discomfort of my uneasy perch on the red hot gunnel [sic] of the lifeboat.

"Shutup."

"Stow it."

"Keep that loony quiet or I'll bash his teeth in."

But the majority of the man's comrades—sixty-five of them, herded together in a boat designed for thirty—sat silent and apathetic, worn down by the heat and the strain, their faces wooden in their weariness.

"I can't stand it . . . I won't. Damn you, I won't. I've got more guts than the lot of you . . . I'm NOT GOING TO WAIT."

His voice broke in a half sob, he jumped to his feet, the secret terror that had lain in him since the shells of *Devonshire* had sliced his comrade into a mass of blood and skin, now triggered

Atlantis: The Story of a German Raider by Ulrich Mohr, as told to A. V. Sellwood (London; Werner Laurie, 1955).

off, exploding into violence. His face was contorted, swollen and red. His eyes were burning, their lids puffed and smarting with the heat and the brine. He swayed as he shouted at us. "Creeping death . . . you can have it. . . . It's me for the drink!" And he turned to the side.

"Stop him," I shouted, then. "You maniac, don't do it."

But even as I shouted the man had jumped.

"My God," said someone. "He's gone."

He fought us with all the strength of the lunatic, spitting out curses and salt water, and clawing at the arms that reached out to save him, until, all fury spent, he lay limp, inert and whimpering in the well of the boat.

"Poor devil," said a seaman.

"Poor devil you say! Be damned for that," I said, and grabbing the would-be suicide by the shoulders I shook him back to coherence. "You useless bastard," I bawled. "Who the hell do you think you are—the only shipwrecked sailor in the world? Try that again and I'll take you at your word and leave your stinking jellied carcass to the sharks."

Passions were running as hot as the sun that set the sea asteam, the sea that with ominous boding of a waiting and open grave dug outside a sick man's window. Wearily I climbed back to my place, linking again the sweating arm of a comrade, a comrade asleep within seconds of the disturbance's ending, and swaying backwards towards the sea. We on the side of the boat sat in line, arms linked in a human chain we had formed for safety . . . dozing, nodding and swaying . . . each man subconsciously alert to jerk his fellow back should he lose balance in his stupor.

We were lucky, very lucky, to have the U-boats with us . . . we were lucky, very lucky . . . But it's difficult, sometimes, to count your blessings when your eyes are swimming with the glare of the sun, and the blood in your head is beating like a hammer, and your stomach is sick, and the wound in your hand is throbbing . . . it's difficult to be philosophic when there are blisters on your seat. . . .

So went the days. Leutnant Fehler had been chosen to command the motor launch and he swept here and there all day long, checking the cables and hurrying up the stragglers when the cables broke. He carried the soup and coffee from the submarines to the boats. He carried the messages for Rogge to the boats and for the boats to the submarines.

Fehler's wardroom nickname had been given him because of his enthusiasm for anything explosive, and now as he went as nursemaid through the little fleet, sleeping little and worrying much, they all called him by that name—Dynamite, Dynamite the shepherd, the waiter, the telegraph boy.

The U-boats were moving north-northwest and Admiral Doenitz, commander of U-boats for the German navy, was informed of the new development.

Actually, Admiral Doenitz had already taken action when he learned that *Raider 16* was sunk, and what happened next was really a result of the sinking of *Raider 16* rather than of *Python*.

On hearing the news Doenitz had ordered Korvettenkapitän Jochen Mohr to take *U-124* to the area. He also ordered Korvettenkapitän Nico Clausen to take *U-129* to Captain Rogge's assistance. (En route, *U-124* encountered the British cruiser HMS *Dunedin*, 240 miles north of the St Paul's rock on the northeast corner of Brazil, and sank that British ship.)

So the two U-boats were heading toward the area where *Raider 16* had gone down anyhow. On the night of December 2, Doenitz issued new orders to the two U-boats, directing them to go with all possible speed to intercept the course of *UA* and *U-68* and take on part of the survivors.

Soon the survivors had worked out a sensible routine. One-third were below decks in the submarines at all times. Another third were in the rubber boats on deck, wearing lifejackets and worrying lest the U-boats dive and leave them stranded. One-third were in the lifeboats. Then, regularly, they switched. The lifeboat men went into the rubber boats, the rubber boat men went below, and the men lording it safely below went into the lifeboats. During these changeovers, Rogge and his officers drilled the men in emergency procedures: the submarines made ready to dive, the rubber boats were floated off, and the lifeboats cast off their tows.

On December 3, *U-129* reached the flotilla and took off Korvettenkapitän Lueders and nearly all the crew of *Python*. Since the U-boat was short of fuel, Rogge decided to keep her with the little fleet and await developments.

Korvettenkapitän Eckermann again proved to be a thoroughly immature young man, chafing under unusual authority. That afternoon he sighted a merchant ship far away. The day before, Merten in *U-68* had seen a ship, but had taken the position that Admiral Doenitz wanted these survivors delivered home and that was his basic responsibility, so he had passed the chance for a shot. Not so Eckermann. He cast off his rubber boats and cast off his lifeboats, and gave chase to the merchantman. He did not catch the other ship or even have a chance to fire a torpedo.

When he came back, a pained Rogge put into effect the change in plan he had now evolved. The smaller ship's boats were scuttled and *U-68* and *UA* each took one of the big steel cutters in tow, while Fehler continued to operate the motorboat independently.

Rogge was growing worried about *U-124*, which was supposed to appear at the same time that *U-129* had reached them. *UA* and *U-68* had been transmitting their position constantly on the Africa wavelength used by the Germans, and Rogge was, as usual, growing worried about this use of radio when the British were so good at direction finding from radio beams. He remarked that it would be very easy for the British to send out a force and make mincemeat of them.

Captain Rogge found it hard to control his fleet. *UA* began transmitting continuous beacon signals (which made Rogge wince) and signaled their position, but made an error in estimate. *U-68* came in with the proper position, to confuse matters; and then asked *U-124* to state *her* position.

U-124 simply did not reply.

Not getting an answer, Rogge began to believe that *U-124* had been sunk, and laid plans to go on without her help, taking all the men from the lifeboats into the three U-boats, no matter how bad the crowding. They simply could not go on like this, making 6 or 7 knots, because the weather was bound to change, and it was doubtful if the half-ship, half-boat flotilla could survive even a moderate blow.

The confusion continued, with messages flying thickly between the rescue force and Admiral Doenitz's command in France. On December 5, Rogge stayed in approximately the same spot all day, for they had reached a point near where the *Dunedin* was sunk, and he could not see how *U-124* could be any further north of them if Mohr had been making an attempt to find them. As they waited, Rogge perfected his plan of moving the 100 men from the open boats into the submarines.

He would act at noon on December 6—they could not wait any longer.

On the night of December 5, *U-124* showed up, Korvetten-kapitän Mohr quite unaware that he had been the cause of much anxiety. He had been going about his U-boat commander's business, making his way toward this area but not neglecting his targets. He had never heard any of the messages sent him, but he was ready to take on his share of survivors. Rogge was angry and dressed Korvettenkapitän Mohr down for causing the men to spend two extra nights in lifeboats, but that was the end of the matter.

Then came the question of fuel. Eckermann in *UA* had plenty of fuel, but he would not give any of it up to the others. *U-68* was short, but she gave 50 tons of fuel to *U-129*. The men were divided up among the U-boats, and the lifeboats and motorboat were sunk. On the night of December 5, *UA* and *U-129* headed toward France on separate courses, and on the morning of December 6, the other two boats set out. Each boat carried 100 extra men. It was to be a unique rescue attempt—if it worked.

In *U-68*, Rogge's boat, the crowding was so intense that the eight officers from *Raider 16* shared the bunk of the officer of the watch, and otherwise spent their time huddled in the tiny wardroom, which Mohr said must have been built to accommodate four very small officers instead of eight very large ones. They used the "hot bed" technique, with each officer occupying a bed for ninety minutes and then getting up so someone else could have it. Mohr finally found a nest under the wardroom table, sleeping on the steel deck, with his lifejacket for a pillow, and with Ferry, Captain Rogge's dog, sleeping on top of him.

Somehow they managed. Somehow the good-natured crew of *U-68* managed to put up with them. Somehow the watches were kept and the meals were cooked on a very small stove—meals for 150 men per day. It was crowded and it was hot—the temperature in the U-boat stood above 96°F. But they survived.

On December 8, Seaman Vicovari, the American who had been wounded on *ZamZam*, was officially notified that he was a prisoner of war. He was sitting on the wooden seat encircling the machine gun on the conning tower at the moment.

On December 12, Admiral Doenitz's headquarters ordered the rescuing U-boats to rendezvous sometime after December 13 off the Cape Verde Islands. There they met four Italian submarines.

Adjutant Mohr went aboard the *Tazzoli*—Rogge sending him with a separate set of *Raider 16*'s records, just in case something happened to *U-68*. Rogge stayed aboard *U-68*, but others went onto *Finzi*, *Calvi*, and *Torelli*. The last headed home, ran into a depth charge attack, and arrived first at St. Nazaire, on December 23, damaged but with all hands safe and sound.

U-68 and *UA* arrived at St. Nazaire on Christmas Day, 1941, 655 days after Captain Rogge and his men had left European soil, having covered 110,000 miles, including 1,000 in lifeboats and several thousand in the maws of the submarines. *Tazzoli* arrived that day, *U-129* and *Calvi* came in on December 27, *Finzi* on December 28, and *U-124* on December 29. The whole ship's company of *Raider 16* was brought together at Nantes, and Captain Rogge read his mail, cleaned up, and paraded his men for the last time before the crew was dismissed. On New Year's Day he and his officers left by special train for Berlin, where Grand Admiral Raeder himself received them at the Kaiserhof. Many medals were awarded that day and Captain Rogge received the Oak Leaves to the Knight's Cross of the Iron Cross with diamonds. Small wonder. He had set a new record for sinkings by merchant raiders and a new record for length of continuous service at sea. For his own satisfaction, too, Captain Rogge had behaved himself with a distinction unusual in World War II on either side, *whenever it was possible*. The problem, as these pages indicate in the stories of Rogge's sinkings and the sinkings of the ships beneath him, was that radio, the fast cruiser, and the U-boat combined in World War II to eradicate the last of the gentlemanliness of war at sea. As mechanized warfare had destroyed chivalry on the land years before with the passing of the cavalry, so the U-boat put the finishing touches on gallantry at sea. Rogge's hero, Kapitän zur See Karl Mueller of the *Emden*, was the last of the great gallants, and his ship went down in 1914. More than a quarter of a century later came Kapitän zur See Bernhard Rogge and it must suffice to say that he did the best he could, and in so doing earned the respect of a great number of his enemies, including several of the captains who had the ill-luck to spend weeks and months aboard *Raider 16* as prisoners of war. It is doubtful if there could ever be another exploit like Rogge's.

EPILOGUE

The sinking of *Raider 16* came nearly at the end of the time of the German merchant raiders in World War II. When the survivors of *Raider 16* arrived at St. Nazaire, there was but one single German merchant raider afloat on any sea in the world.

Admiral Raeder did not give up hope for the theory, and more raiders were prepared. *Raider 10* (*Thor*) went out on her second cruise that December and sank 56,000 tons of shipping before she was destroyed by fire. In March, 1943, *Raider 28* (*Michel*) sank 104,000 tons of shipping in the Atlantic and Indian Oceans, but after the war the captain who had accomplished this was tried and sentenced to 16 years in prison for having fired longer than was necessary on three British merchantmen. The character of raiding had changed!

The character of enemy merchant ships became sterner, too. In the spring of 1942, *Raider 23* (*Stier*) encountered the U.S. Liberty Ship *Stephen Hopkins*. Although the *Stephen Hopkins* was destroyed, she set fire to *Raider 23* and forced the German crew to abandon ship.

By this time, 1942, the British made it impossible to send more raiders into the Atlantic. *Raider 45* (*Komet*) tried to go out again after a first successful voyage, but was destroyed by British patrol vessels. *Raider 14* (*Togo*) was so badly damaged in an air attack at Boulogne that she had to return to Germany. *Raider 28* was sunk in the Indian Ocean in 1943 by an American submarine, and the raider program, for all practical purposes, was canceled. One other reason for the cancellation was Hitler's growing irritation with all arms of the navy save the U-boat division, his replacement of Admiral Raeder by Admiral Doenitz as commander in chief of the navy in 1943, and his strict orders that surface ships were to move as little as possible.

Raider 16's campaign, then, marked the high point of German raider operations in both wars. As for Captain Rogge, he was truly a national hero, one of the handful to survive the pitfalls of a losing nation in a desperate war, the postwar recrimination and de-Nazification, and other troubles of the German navy. After the award ceremonies in Berlin, Rogge went onward in the German navy. He was promoted to rear admiral and he fought against the Russians with the Third Battle Group, one of whose major tasks was support of the evacuation of German forces in the Baltic region as the battle went against Germany. At war's end he was vice-admiral, commander of Task Force Rogge, and his flagship was the cruiser *Prinz Eugen*. He was discharged from the navy in 1945 when the German navy was virtually broken up. By the end of 1955, there were only 80 officers and petty officers left in German naval service, and when the North Atlantic Treaty powers decided to recreate a German navy, it was necessary to find and recruit the old officers of World War II. Rear Admiral Rogge was appointed commander of Military District I (Schleswig-Holstein and Hamburg) and NATO commander for the allied land forces from Schleswig-Holstein and Hamburg and he served until March, 1962, when he retired as vice admiral to live near Hamburg and devote his time to the merchant shipping business and to ocean sailing.

NOTES AND BIBLIOGRAPHY

The basic story of Captain Rogge and *Raider 16* (*Atlantis*) was told in Rogge's own book, *Schiff 16*, prepared with the assistance of Wolfgang Frank and published in 1955 by Gerhard Stalling Verlag of Oldenburg and Hamburg. This book was later published in English as *Under Ten Flags*, translated by Lt. Cdr. R. O. B. Long, RNVR, by Weidenfeld and Nicolson of London. The English version is considerably shorter and less detailed than the German. Another important source is *Atlantis: The Story of a German Raider*, by Ulrich Mohr, as told to A. V. Sellwood, published by Werner Laurie, London, in 1955. Mohr also brought out *Die Kriegsfahrt des Hilfskreuzers Atlantis, Bilddokumente einer Kreuzerfahrt in vier Ozeanen*, a book of photographs and captions, published by Verlag die Heimbücherei John Jahr, Berlin. This is most valuable in giving a pictorial background for the cruise of the raider.

Admiral Rogge published an article on his problems of leadership aboard the *Atlantis* in the February, 1963, issue of the *Proceedings* of the United States Naval Institute. Charles J. V. Murphy published a colorful story of the sinking of the *ZamZam* in *Life* magazine in June, 1941, as noted in the text. Extremely valuable in the preparation of *Raider 16* was the volume *War in the Southern Oceans, 1939–45*, part of *The South Africa Prime Minister's Department, Union War Histories Section*, by L. C. F. Turner, H. R. Gordon-Cumming, and J. E. Betzler, published by Oxford University Press in 1961. Other vital sources were the *History of the Second World War, United Kingdom Military Series, The War at Sea, 1939–45*, by Captain S. W. Roskill, DSC, RN, Volume I: *The Defensive*, published by Her Majesty's Stationery Office, London, 1954; *Der Seekrieg, The German Navy's Story*, by Vice Admiral Friedrich Ruge, translated by Cdr. M. G. Saunders, RN, published by the United States Naval Institute, Annapolis, Md., 1957; *Memoirs:*

Ten Years and Twenty Days, by Admiral Karl Doenitz, translated by R. H. Stephens in collaboration with David Woodward, published by The World Publishing Co., Cleveland and New York, 1959; *The Conduct of the War at Sea*, an essay by Admiral Karl Doenitz, published by the Division of Naval Intelligence, January, 1946; the unpublished manuscript *German Surface Ships, Policy and Operations in World War II*, by Eberhard Weichold, vice admiral of the German navy, prepared for the U.S. navy department.

Useful secondary sources included *Swastika at Sea, The Struggle and Destruction of the German Navy, 1939–45*, by C. D. Bekker (pseud.), published by William Kimber, London, 1953; *The Secret Raiders, The Story of the German Armed Merchant Raiders in the Second World War*, by David Woodward, published by W. W. Norton and Co., New York, 1955; *The Sea Raiders*, by Captain Kenneth Langmaid, DSC, RN, published by Jarrold's, London, 1963; and *Hitler's Strategy*, by F. H. Hinsley, Cambridge University Press, 1951.

I am much indebted to librarians at Yale University and at the United States Naval Academy at Annapolis for assistance in securing books and documents; to Edgar Beyn, Jr., of Annapolis and Hamburg for material about Captain Rogge; to Olga G. Hoyt for editorial assistance; and to Mrs. Annette Graves for typing.

INDEX

WORLD WAR II
Edwin P. Hoyt

BOWFIN　　　　　　　　　　**69817-X/$3.50 US/$4.95 Can**

An action-packed drama of submarine-chasing destroyers.

THE MEN OF THE GAMBIER BAY　　**55806-8/$3.50 US/$4.75 Can**

Based on actual logs and interviews with surviving crew members, of the only U.S. aircraft carrier to be sunk by naval gunfire in World War II.

STORM OVER THE GILBERTS:　　**63651-4/$3.50 US/$4.50 Can**
War in the Central Pacific: 1943

The dramatic reconstruction of the bloody battle over the Japanese-held Gilbert Islands.

TO THE MARIANAS:　　　　**65839-9/$3.50 US/$4.95 Can**
War in the Central Pacific: 1944

The Allies push toward Tokyo in America's first great amphibious operation of World War II.

CLOSING THE CIRCLE:　　　**67983-8/$3.50 US/$4.95 Can**
War in the Pacific: 1945

A behind-the-scenes look at the military and political moves drawn from official American and Japanese sources.

McCAMPBELL'S HEROES　　　**68841-7/$3.95 US/$5.75 Can**

A stirring account of the daring fighter pilots, led by Captain David McCampbell, of Air Group Fifteen.

THE SEA WOLVES　　　　**75249-2/$3.50 US/$4.95 Can**

The true story of Hitler's dreaded U-boats of WW II and the allied forces that fought to stop them.

THE CARRIER WAR　　　　**75360-X/$3.50 US/$4.50 Can**

The exciting account of the air and sea battles that defeated Japan in the Pacific.

ALL BOOKS ILLUSTRATED
WITH MAPS AND ACTION PHOTOGRAPHS